The Unofficial Walt Disney World Drinking Companion

Christopher Schmidt

Theme Park Press
The Happiest Books on Earth
www.ThemeParkPress.com

Editor: Bob McLain
Layout: Artisanal Text

ISBN 978-1-68390-092-4
Printed in the United States of America

Theme Park Press | www.ThemeParkPress.com
Address queries to bob@themeparkpress.com

For Elisabeth and Dennis Schmidt, my amazing parents, who are responsible for my Disney and margarita appreciation.

Contents

Author's Note

This may come as a surprise, but there are several hundred different locations within the Walt Disney World Resort where guests may order a beer, cocktail, glass of wine, high-octane smoothie, or ice cream float with booze in it. Time, tide, and Disney theme park expansion wait for no one, and every month, it seems, another dozen outlets pop up on the property.

If I were to offer a complete list of restaurants, bars, kiosks, shops, carts, counters, and pavilion purveyors, and the alcoholic beverage offerings at each, this guide would necessarily resemble a weighty stack of menus. Informative, surely, though the repetition could prove tedious, and would leave little space for scintillating commentary. It would also be out of date as soon as it was printed.

My mission, then, is to offer a pointed examination of every Walt Disney World drinking venue and opportunity, and capture the particular charm of each. The guide's particular emphasis surrounds enjoyment, entertainment, and exhaustive exploration of the glorious lounge, patio, and pool bars, rather than a repetitive recount of every available beverage.

Generally, for those interested to know what drinks can be found where, fairly comprehensive detail is provided. However, so that my more exacting readers won't throw this guide into Seven Seas Lagoon in frustration at the forty-fifth Piña CoLAVA mention, more space is afforded to theme, character, and unique, wonderful potables, rather than a complete rehash of every beer, wine, and cocktail.

Many highlighted beverages betray a specific personal preference. However, as every available India Pale Ale is not exclusively featured, familiar readers will note I did manage to somewhat rein in my partiality. At any rate, the mere mention of even a single whiskey drink reveals my infallible objectivity.

Introduction

An incredible amount of good fortune surrounds the creation and publication of a Disney drinking guide. This being the second of two such guides, I am doubly grateful for the people and forces that have contributed to turning this incredible opportunity into a companion-volume reality.

In part, I wish to show my gratitude by imploring every Disney enthusiast I can influence to conduct themselves as adults. Such admonition applies to life in general, and as it regards behavior within a Disney-fashioned family resort, most especially. Unless you happen to be an actual child. In which case, put this book down and go ride some rides, would ya?

The privilege of enjoying a Berry Bellini on a fountain-festooned Epcot patio, or the world's most delectable IPA on the top floor of the Contemporary Resort, is as enviable as it may be fleeting. Disney is delighted to make the kind of margin afforded by alcohol sales. Still, Disney is, above all else, an entertainment company. They understand it is the mouse, creatively themed roller coasters, and prestige that bring in the masses. Surely, the parks attract a few more people, a little more often, since a certain demographic has fairly easy access to alcohol. You can be equally sure, Disney would mothball every wine bar, beer stein, and margarita machine if they measured a dip in attendance by those who don't drink (see families), as any result of those who do.

Instances of purely poor park behavior are, fortunately for us all, relatively rare; at least when compared to anywhere in the real world. If we could convince ourselves not to engage in the truly foolhardy "Drinking Around the World" pursuit, incidents might well be negligible.

What I endeavor to impart is how additionally wonderful a Walt Disney World visit can be with a glass of wine before the parade, or a poolside fruity Grey Goose concoction. Magic abounds for everyone when no one is subjected to, or experiencing, the negative effects of compulsive alcohol consumption.

Have a drink. You're meant to. Alcohol wouldn't be available throughout Walt Disney World otherwise. Enjoy less than your absolute limit, and let everyone within your circle of influence enjoy their day.

CHAPTER ONE

Epcot

This chapter just happens to be organized in the manner one would, though should not, approach Epcot if one so happened to be Drinking Around the World. Drinking or otherwise, guests ought to start in the Mexico Pavilion and proceed clockwise around the lagoon until you get to Canada, and back to the Showcase Plaza—more accurately, for you compulsive drinkers, until you fall down somewhere near Japan, and pray you have worthwhile friends to Dasani-water you back to health (though if they were any kind of friends at all, they would either have stopped you, or would be falling apart along with you).

Mexico

Everyone has a favorite pavilion. For me, Mexico ranks at the top as it has everything: exceptional food, incredible cocktails, a Mayan pyramid inside of a larger Mayan pyramid, and a Donald-Duck-heavy attraction, the Three Caballeros Gran Fiesta Tour, which is a little dated and maybe culturally primitive, even insensitive. But it's a dark ride, drifts for seven minutes through air-conditioned paradise, and Donald Duck is my favorite classic Disney character. So we can overlook a bit of stereotyping.

The pavilion itself is home to the best collection of cantinas and cocinas this side of the real Mexico.

La Cantina de San Angel

As far as I may rely on my limited Spanish, this patio walk-up counter presents a moderate misnomer. Cantina, to me, always meant bar. This location does serve alcohol in a few forms, though there is no bar to either lean against, nor from which to order. There are no cantineros (bartenders). Most importantly, to the designation, there are none of the requisite free chips and salsa that accompanies any cantina worthy of my patronage.

Despite confusion, and scarcity of free chips, La Cantina de San Angel is lovely. This particular patio is often a reliable place to find a table when other portions of the park have succumbed to common crowding (see, especially, La Cava del Tequila, below). A covered, yet open-air dining area welcomes guests, with a ring of tables right on the water. With the view, lagoon-bolstered breeze, and frequency of shaded tables, I am always surprised to find a seat here.

A Modelo or margarita on this patio will help you forget you paid for chips. This is not a criticism, but with the margarita selection to be had at every other dining location in the Mexico Pavilion, I rarely order a drink from La Cantina, specifically. An Avión on the rocks, at a table on the rail, is wonderful. If you can get into La Cava, and still want La Cantina's atmosphere, grab a far, far superior margarita there, and come back out for the sunshine and people watching here.

Notable Potables

Avión Fresh Lime on the Rocks
Splendid, but for the price (a pomegranate liqueur floater is extra), you will do much better at the other cantinas

Modelo Especial
16 oz. draft

La Cava del Tequila

If you have any mind at all for drinking at Epcot, then you are surely aware of La Cava del Tequila. La Cava has a bit of a cult following. It's the type of place regulars return with religious adherence. Food, drink, charm, and service-wise, the place is just incredible. It is several layers of popular, and often difficult to get into, in the way Gran Fiesta Tour is not.

For those who appreciate a fine sipping-tequila, and desire it for reasons others don't need to understand at a family amusement park, this is the perfect place to get and enjoy it. Those who like a sweeter-than-sin mixed drink, in remarkable hues and curious combinations of fruit and cactus liquor, well, this is also the place for that.

Certain alcohol purists and fly-by-night frothy-fruit drinkers don't always mesh. The utterly professional cast members within La Cava del Tequila serve as the bridge spanning this significant gap. All are welcome, and treated with smiling courtesy and genuine respect. This is as it should be. Surrounded by magic, wonder, and hand-crafted happiness, an honest difference in taste ought not divide us. Watching a guest mix Don Julio into his Michelada-style chaser, rather than drinking them separately, was hard to endure. I was warmed, by tequila, surely, and the fact that no one threw chips at him.

Notable Potables

La Cava Tequila Flights
I personally don't go this route. Three shots of tequila, no matter the quality, do not comfortably compliment my vision of a Walt Disney World visit. If you are a sipper, or have amigos with whom to share such delicacies, flights may suit you, and La Cava maintains an extraordinary inventory

Wild Passion Fruit Margarita
Tequila, ginger liqueur, passion fruit, mango, and fresh lime juice, topped with mango foam, and on the rocks with a Tajín chili powder rim

Choza de Margarita

A new tequileria and margarita bar coming to the Mexico Pavilion in late 2017. With the construction fencing between La Cantina and the pyramid, we know it will be an outdoor facility. Due to La Cava's overwhelming success, this move is necessary and Disney-brilliant. I can't wait to go back and see it.

La Hacienda de San Angel

It's La Cantina de San Angel without the potential sun exposure. Truly, La Hacienda is quite a bit different, though the incredible view is the same. La Hacienda is slightly more elegant, the menu is larger and more refined, and you get wonderful table service. There are several more margaritas available, and, I should have said this first, you get free chips and salsa.

The menu and service are similar to what you would find inside the pyramid, at San Angel Inn. What's lacking is the breathtaking and intimate inside-the-pyramid setting. What you gain is a far greater chance of getting a table. This doesn't mean La Hacienda isn't independently wonderful. It's just that your restaurante either has a volcano and boat ride going through it, or it does not.

Notable Potables

Lime Raspberry Margarita
Rancho alegre 100% agave premium reposado Tequila, orange liqueur, raspberry puree, fresh lime juice, and agave nectar syrup, served on the rocks

Rosita Margarita
Exótico 100% agave premium silver tequila, orange liqueur, fresh lime juice and rose infusions, served on the rocks with hibiscus Himalayan salt rim

San Angel Inn Restaurante

You know that feeling you get, or at least half the people around you get, when you ride the Pirates of the Caribbean attraction during the day, and forget it's still light outside? The sensation is even more glorious if you take lunch inside the Mexico Pavilion, at San Angel Inn Restaurante.

It's a little pricey. The place you walk past on your way home from a night on the town is about one-tenth as expensive. That place isn't adorned with Mayan pyramids, active volcanoes, and a Donald Duck attraction, though. San Angel is fairly time and labor-intensive if all you're looking for is a cocktail. The same beverage selection is available elsewhere in the pavilion. It's the experience that's impossible to replicate.

If you have the time for a full, flavorful meal, with all the environmental trimmings, San Angel is well worth the invest-ment. I recently discovered the dish I loved as a youngster has chorizo in it. I wonder if my parents knew. They certainly didn't tell me. I was a bit of a capricious eater. They wouldn't have risked eliminating something else from my menu.

Named in honor of the former Norwegian attraction in the neighboring pavilion, San Angel's Maelstrom margarita is a thrill ride in a glass. It is not for the faint of heart, or taste buds. I don't usually enjoy habanero, though Maelstrom brings enough flavor to help mask the brutality. Plus, anything with Tajín in or on it becomes that much more palatable.

Notable Potables

Maelstrom
Tequila Milagro blanco, mango puree, orange liqueur, habanero peppers, blueberries, and basil, with a Tajín chili powder rim

Michelada
Mexican draft beer, tomato-clam juice, orange juice, and lime juice, Worcestershire sauce, Maggi seasoning, Valentina, and soy sauces

Norway

When the adorable, air-conditioned Maelstrom attraction shut its doors, a loyal, vocal Disney contingent created quite an uproar; at least, in their corner of the world. As Frozen Ever After continues to draw hourly crowds, which Maelstrom didn't see in a weekend, the Disney decision-makers stand resolutely vindicated.

Norway's attraction is not its food. If you can name a Norwegian drink, you are more culturally savvy than most. It is still charming, and still worth a visit, even if you can't ride Frozen and don't have reservations for an Akershus character meal.

Akershus Royal Banquet Hall

There are three kinds of people in this world: (1) the type who can't imagine drinking at a Disney character-dining restaurant, (2) those who can't imagine eating at one without a drink, and (3) those who can drink there, but don't eat, nor have children.

I identify strongly with group 2. The people from the first group could lighten up a bit. As for the latter, seek professional psychological, social, and likely, medical help. If the rules of your particular Drinking Around the World competition call for you to grab a round from the Akershus character breakfast, throw in the towel before you hurt yourself. Plus, it's this type of behavior that validates the reactionary bigotry of Group 1.

Disney Parks and Resorts serve alcohol. I bring it up constantly; perhaps it's a defense mechanism. If we weren't meant to drink, we wouldn't be able to acquire drinks so easily. Truly, Akershus isn't an "easy" place to get a drink, what with the supposition you will have a meal, and a family. If you can get your ducks in a row, and get a table, the venue is positively glorious, and the specialty drinks menu is as creative as anything in Epcot, which is saying a lot.

The Frozen-themed cocktails are charming enough to order. They are also brimming with ingredients with which you may not be familiar. Aquavit is a traditional Scandinavian liqueur, made popular by long-suffering slogging through interminable winters. At a Disney World restaurant, mixed into a glass with raspberries, it's as undesirable and out of place as Josh Gad in a live-action romance. The drinks on the specialty menu, and those highlighted below, are delightful, in theory. I dare you to drink one, and defy you to like it (coffee drinks excepted; they're wonderful).

Notable Potables

The Kristiansand
Taste Norway's southern coast with a frozen combination of raspberries, mango, Linie Aquavit, and rum

The Oslo
This frozen, fruity favorite combines strawberries with crème de banana, Linie Aquavit, and vodka

Kringla Bakeri Og Kafe

If you don't have kids, or someone keen to get a Frozen FastPass+, this may be the only part of the Norway Pavilion you see. The sandwiches are reasonable, if a tad bland for those used to eighteen ingredients and spicy peppers on everything.

Get a pastry instead. There are a number of chocolate and custard options, plus something called cloudberry. They're all delicious, as long as you don't outsmart yourself and try the lefse, a potato pancake. Whoever first called these pancakes has a twisted sense of humor.

The pastries pair wonderfully with Kringla's alcoholic coffee drinks, with wine, even with Carlsberg. The Kafe also serves

Aquavit. Don't fall for that either. It's a good way to ruin everything else you order, even the fake pancake.

Notable Potables

Viking Coffee
Flavored with Kamora Coffee Liqueur and Baileys Irish Cream

Carlsberg beer
16 oz. draft

Norway Frozen Treats Cart

When you arrive to find the wait time on your phone is incorrect, and the 25-minute line for Frozen, which you were prepared to tolerate, is truly 55 minutes, take solace in this convenient outdoor vendor. It will have a much more manageable line.

There are a number of beers you've likely never heard of, a few wines that you probably have, and our old friend Aquavit. Let me describe this noxious sludge, since it keeps coming up. Are you familiar with Jägermeister? Imagine Jägermeister mixed with Nyquil, in an even less appetizing yellow hue. If you order an Aquavit, especially in shot form, I recommend you pour it directly on your shoes. This cuts out the interim effort of drinking it, then throwing it up.

Notable Potables

Einstöck Toasted Porter
16 oz. draft

Einstöck White Ale
16 oz. draft

China

I mentioned earlier that the Mexico Pavilion is my favorite. In large part, this is due to the cuisine and charm. Everything in World Showcase is charming. Every pavilion offers incredible, authentic eats. It's inaccurate to say I don't love Chinese, Italian, Moroccan food, etc. Fact is, I am *most* partial to Mexican food and margaritas. The life-sized hacienda diorama with a market, volcano, tequila bar, and boat ride inside is also hard to beat.

The China Pavilion is beautiful. The food and frozen concoctions are terrific. It takes nothing away from China, nor any other pavilion, that I like Mexico better. Not satisfied? When your favorite pavilion puts in a boat ride, and some better food than Norway, we'll talk.

Joy of Tea

This delightful outdoor vendor sits on the shores of the lagoon. You may not be aware of it. It's easy to miss as your attention is drawn by the spectacle of the pavilion itself, in the opposite direction. This is a shame, as it is an excellent place to grab a quick, reasonable, tasty snack and cocktail.

I can't recommend passing on any of the more authentic fare to be had elsewhere to come here for egg rolls. On any given Saturday, when you're desperate for some place without a prohibitive line, Joy of Tea is the outlet for all your oddly named, conceived, and tasting treats.

Joy of Tea serves Bubble Tea; the persistent, ineffable sensation. I still can't get used to firing balls of gelatin into my brain through an oversized straw, but the kids seem to love it. As bizarre as Bubble Tea is, it is skim milk compared to Joy of Tea's Tipsy Ducks cocktail. Bourbon, coffee, black tea, and chocolate? It's probably quite the pick-me-up. I won't know until they hand out samples of it for free.

Good thing, for your stomach, the only close attraction is Frozen, and you aren't getting on that anyway. Be sure to watch the expression of the expatriates working the counter when you order this drink by name. Be sure also not to get one on your way to Test Track, or the orange version of Mission Space.

Notable Potables

Tipsy Ducks in Love
Bourbon, coffee, black tea, cream, and chocolate syrup

Tsing Tao Beer
16 oz. draft

Lotus Blossom Café

Every culture has a wealth of undiscovered delicacies, just waiting to thrill visitors. China is no exception. When I look at the Lotus Blossom menu, I cannot help but think Disney's reliably brilliant creative minds dropped the Baoding ball.

Tsing Tao and plum wine; delightful. Each ring with cultural authenticity, and strike a chord for most westerners. But then, Yuengling and Bud Light? Yuengling is served copiously throughout Epcot, so it's presence here falls short of being due to its cynically Chinese-sounding name. I have a petty, personal Bud Light hangup, which is well documented. There is nothing wrong with either beer, but ought they be beer choice #2 and #3 at a Chinese restaurant?

My advice, if you absolutely must have a drink here? Get a mango or strawberry smoothie, and a plum wine, then combine them. My sincere advice, don't do this. Take your ten dollars in either direction along the esplanade, where you will find many, much better options.

Notable Potables

Tsing Tao Beer
12 oz. bottle

Plum Wine

Nine Dragons Restaurant

If you are keen to have an excellent meal with your culturally interesting cocktail, Nine Dragons is mere steps and a world of apart from Lotus Blossom. I keep harping on that; it's just so rare when you find something on a Disney property that is so inescapably unspectacular. I know, it is because Disney sets the bar so high, and it's what makes Disney so special. When you come across something that's just so-so, like Lotus Blossom, it really stands out.

Nine Dragons, and a hundred other eateries around the resort, stand out as well—giving the opposite impression, for reasons much more reliably Disney. Superior service, setting, offerings, atmosphere; all the things you come to expect, and perhaps take for granted. Nine Dragons has them all.

I try not to behave as if I am cooler than anyone else. I do, however, shy away from what I consider a fad. I have never owned an iPhone. I didn't wear cargo shorts. I stayed mostly clear of the mojito craze. This latter is not due to any objection to the drinks themselves. I was a bartender when they became popular, and it's a total pain to make a proper one.

That said, I do love the currently popular "Mule" drinks: the Moscow Mule, Black Cherry Mule, even the Kentucky Mule. Nine Dragons has its own version. They call it a Ginger Zinger. I don't favor rum with flavored soda drinks these days; my brain and body find the combination too sweet. Ginger ale works its own particular magic. I will admit, again, to not being a purist. Pretty much any drink that isn't working for me can be fixed with ginger ale. That's sacrilege to martini drinkers. If you're being completely honest with yourself, I bet that straight whatever you ordered would be far more pleasurable with some Schweppes in it.

Then, Nine Dragons presents something called Heavenly Clouds. I enthusiastically credit the Epcot creative contingent for their wonderful, thoughtful concoctions. Around the World Showcase, and at every annual festival, specialty drinks menus are simply bristling with irresistible new pleasures. Then you come across something like this, and you wonder who called out sick that day.

Guests' tastes are not all the same. I don't expect everyone to love margaritas, Bloody Marys, and IPA the way I do. Everyone should, though I know it's not practical. But who, I ask you, craves a glass full of three disparate fruit flavors with heavy cream in it?

Don't get me wrong; I appreciate coconut and pineapple, together. I rarely drink it, now that I order drinks like an adult, though it does not offend me. Nor does the thought of cream in a beverage. In deference to what I just said about adulthood, there are numerous Dreamsicle variations I am quite fond of. Melon liqueur, too, is eminently drinkable, in the right mix. This ain't it.

There's just too much going on in the glass. No matter how you feel at the time, the first sip gives you the sensation of trying to force in dessert after you've eaten too much dinner. Even if your palate can process the flavor storm, this creamy, sweet-and-sour hurricane will do a disservice to your stomach. I mentioned earlier not having the Bourbon-chocolate-coffee drink before going on Test Track. With Heavenly Clouds in your system, I wouldn't even go on Spaceship Earth.

Notable Potables

Ginger Zinger
Ginger liqueur, light rum, ginger ale, lemon twist

Heavenly Clouds
Coconut rum, honeydew melon liqueur, pineapple juice, cream float

Outpost

Outpost is its own pavilion, despite a number of nations vying for this space. The holdup may have to do with how much of the Illuminations equipment is stored directly behind the esplanade in this area. I love Illuminations. Wouldn't want them to change a thing. Certainly don't want to see it go. Can't they maybe dock the huge globe behind the Odyssey Center, and give us a Brazil, or India, or some other missing culture?

Refreshment Cool Post

Two words: Frozen Elephant. If you are going to stop at the Outpost, either as part of a Drinking Around the World contest, or because other parts of the park are starting to suffer significant lines, a Frozen Elephant is what you need.

As a kid, who didn't love an enormous slushy? Sometimes you got cherry. Occasionally you tried the blue stuff. More often than not, though, you wanted a good old-fashioned cup full of frozen Coke. Well, the Outpost has that, and they've got something much, much better; at least for adults. Loaded with Amarula Cream Liqueur, a Coke slush takes on a slight caramel flavor, with delightfully alcoholic after-effects.

The Outpost possesses a couple of the very few umbrella-covered tables in World Showcase. The Cool Post itself has a tiny covered patio surrounded by rather effective fans. When your timing is right, this is a nice area to sit for a bit. If you are unfortunate, a group of kids, or a roving band of drunks who have broken off from Drinking Around the World, have discovered the noisome percussion instruments. Someone must have thought this would lend positively to the Outpost's modest cultural expression. What it does is create an auditory crime scene. I am all for people having fun, so rather than scowl or complain, I tend to take my beverage and move on.

Notable Potables

Frozen Elephant
Frozen Coca-Cola and Amarula Cream Liqueur

Old Elephant Foot IPA
16 oz. draft

Germany

Candy, foul-smelling food, and beer you can't pronounce and probably won't like. That's the impression many have of modern-day Germany. Disney certainly does its part in perpetuating it. The Germany Pavilion is as charming as any other. I love it, especially the caramel shop and miniature village. But it is absolutely not some place I choose to eat. Ever. And that's hard to admit, as most of my ancestors are from there (see "Schmidt").

I know I am a huge disappointment. I am just not a wurst/loaf/schnitzel kind of guy. And sauerkraut? I'm not apologizing for loathing sauerkraut. It's spoiled cabbage. Perfect cabbage is only slightly worth eating. No one of sound mind should purposely put sauerkraut into their mouth. The smell alone ought to ward you off. In describing the worst sandwich he can imagine, Dr. Seuss equates sauerkraut with toadstools and arsenic. So, it ain't just me. Come for the beer and character. Shy away from everything else.

Bier

It's not on the map. It does not appear on the Walt Disney World online dining page. It is, however, in the shade at the right time, and when it has a line, it moves fairly well—not as well as the Space Mountain FastPass+ line, but better surely than Sommerfest, and you don't want to be in that line anyway.

Between this and the bier cart on the walkway, two of the three best places to stop in Germany aren't included in the promo materials. The third is Karamell-Küche, the candy store.

Ten dollars is pretty steep for a soft pretzel, though this one is huge. Interested in German beer? I can only prescribe the pilsner, Warsteiner. Then, yeah, you're going to want the pretzel, too. They complement one another.

Take your authentic bounty and stroll over to the spectacular, rustic German village mockup, on the esplanade. Disneyland has a Storybook Land attraction, which takes guests through model miniaturizations of classic Disney-adopted fairytales. My wife and kids think it's boring, so I don't get to enjoy it like I want to. I have to travel to Walt Disney World by myself now to see anything similar. This isn't quite the same, though it is entirely charming. If you view it from the right angle, you can lose yourself in the creative precision.

Notable Potables

Warsteiner Dunkel
20 oz. draft

Bärenjäger Honey & Bourbon Shot

Biergarten Restaurant

A slice of paradise on earth. This is exactly what one longs for and expects when Disney's creative forces put their hands and minds to something. It's got the rare, romantic, outdoor night-time feel, similar to Pirates of the Caribbean and the Mexico Pavilion. The level of and attention to detail instantly transports you to a quaint, comfortable, familiar German village, even for those who have never traveled there.

High-energy, traditional performances thrill diners from the twilit, tree-lined theatre; Biergarten's centerpiece. The Von Trapp children (yes, I know that was in Austria) load your table with platters of food, and will beam with genuine warmth, even as you unconsciously mock their accent.

If the place wasn't weighed down with the odor of inedible pottage, I would pay to stay in one of the rooms above the stage. I know people love it; you need reservations most days just to get in. I want to love it, I really do. There are just certain smells, flavors, and sensations certain of us can't get past. For me, it's most of whatever is going on in the Biergarten kitchen.

Making a further mess of the situation, I also don't favor the Bavarian style of beer. This pains me most of all. I love the very idea of Oktoberfest. Yet, give me a beer with diaeresis in the name, and my nose starts running. I do like pilsner, as long as it isn't overly aromatic. Blasphemy, I know.

My squeamishness is not universal. Nor should it stop anyone from enjoying this spectacular and memorable experience. Eat and drink at your discretion. I have little expertise in the matter. Try the wine, maybe. Being geographically bracketed by France and Italy all those millennia has to be worth something.

Notable Potables

August Kesseler Pinot Noir
Glass/Bottle

Schöfferhofer Pink Grapefruit Hefeweizen
Half-liter/Liter draft

Sommerfest

All the olfactory presence of Biergarten, with little of the charm or atmosphere. I feel this walk-up counter was established to appease guests who couldn't get into Biergarten, and is indeed in its shadow, in every respect.

I have been shut out of a restaurant I love. It would have gone a long way toward salvaging my day and mood had there been a replica quick-service option right next door. I imagine Sommerfest is serving this purpose.

There's one thing I would ever get from here, personally: a Bärenjäger Honey & Bourbon shot. Yet, I still won't do it. They sell it at the bier window outside, and the bier cart on the esplanade, in the much, much fresher air. Without reservations for, or just to take a look at the Biergarten, I can't even see a reason to come back here.

Italy

We depart the Germany Pavilion, where the atmosphere is delightful, though fine fare is rare, and come to Italy, a pavilion that is a victim of its culture's surfeit of wonderful food. The Italy Pavilion is so impacted with excellent restaurants, snack counters, and wine bars, there's no room for anything else.

There is a fountain. Some statuary. Gondolas. Flowers. A burro pulling a cart. And, of course, a smoking section. There is, however, nothing to do but take photos of these things, and eat. It's not a knock on Italy, or Morocco (we will discuss this later; Morocco is mostly food-based, also). I just wish Epcot housed a few more dark rides with little boats in them.

Enoteca Castello

A wine shop that pours vino for your immediate gratification is a wine bar. One would surmise, a wine shop, or bar, within the splendor of Epcot's Italy Pavilion would attach a prohibitive markup to its products. This is not the case. Enoteca is not giving wine away, though $6 (at press time) for a glass of cultural marvel, or any of several $15 flights, feels like a steal.

There aren't enough tables outside the glorious little shop. I almost feel guilty bringing my Via Napoli calamari over here. An eager Banfi purchase sufficiently cures that. With everything there is to see, and do, within Walt Disney World, guests are often compelled to rush about, in an attempt to see, and do, everything. No matter how often I visit, or for however many days, I can't stop myself from attempting to overdo it.

The raised cocktail tables on the esplanade present an ideal opportunity to take a minute. Do it. Sure, you can easily make your way through much of the American Adventure in those fifteen minutes, but it'll still be there fifteen minutes from now. Relax. Deliberately enjoy a glass of wine. Take your time. Experiencing Epcot at leisure, within a wine-fostered comfort cloud, ought to be preferable to a high-pressure haste haze. I wish I could remind myself to do it more often.

Notable Potables
Italian Liqueur Shots
Orangecello, Limoncello

Red, White, Rose, Sparkling Wine Flights

Gelati

Gelati presents as a simple ice cream cart. It's in Italy, though, so it vends about a dozen different wines and Italian beers. It also sells gelato. The line often rivals Frozen Ever After. Anytime you can grab a quick Chianti on your way along the esplanade, you will be having a good day. This is rarely possible without facing the aforementioned gelato-ravenous line. Fortunately, there are many other places to find beer, wine, and dolce.

Notable Potables

Bellini
Peach puree and Prosecco

Moretti La Rossa
12 oz. bottle

Tutto Gusto Wine Cellar

A wine lounge, inside Epcot's Italy Pavilion. If you don't have the time or inclination to stay awhile, I recommend you stay away. Tutto Gusto will draw you in, comfort, and then confine you in its welcoming, if relentless embrace. Fortunately, and this is something I never say, the furniture is not that comfortable, or plentiful, or I would be getting constantly kicked out of this place.

This is Italy's answer to La Cava del Tequila, and I wish all the pavilions would follow suit. The Rose & Crown is another fine example of a delightfully Disney-fashioned, cultural watering hole. Every pavilion could use one. I don't know what a local tavern would look like in Norway, though I would love to play shuffleboard at a Disney dive bar by America Gardens Theatre.

Tutto Gusto offers several hundred wines, meat and cheese pairings that would impress the Pope, and full specialty entrées and desserts. I'm telling you, if it were on the water, I would try to move here.

It seems like a sin to order anything other than wine—though as I say, if we weren't meant to have what's offered, they wouldn't offer it. The fine people at Budweiser would probably appreciate it if I applied this philosophy to their product, and stop complaining about the presence of Bud Light everywhere. Yes, the Italy Pavilion is swimming with Bud Light. Just like the real world Italy, no?

Notable Potables

Moretti La Rossa
20 oz. draft

Florida Craft Brews
16 oz. draft, rotating

Tutto Italia Ristorante

The crown jewel of, arguably, Epcot's culinary capital. France, Canada, Japan, and others all make a case for having Epcot's finest restaurant. Universally, only Mexico competes with Italy for comprehensive food quality. And while I love the San Angel venues, what we're having here is a five-star discussion.

It takes a reservation to get in, unless you like waiting hours for a table; the table where you will be sure to be struck by both the kitchen and bathroom doors. You should also dress up a bit. Despite the effort, you should eat here, at least once in your life. Price, decadence, and the associated ordeal (dress code) keep me from recommending a restaurant such as this. But everyone should at least see it.

Surrounded by such wonder, immerse yourself in the splendor and culture. Tutto has spaghetti. It has lasagna. They are both wonderful. Don't order either. Tutto offers the opportunity to try, and love, something you have never had. Everything on the menu is incredible, so you aren't taking much of a chance. Look at the other tables on the way in, or ask your server what exactly is it that smells so darn good (don't say it like that).

I feel differently about cocktails. I am willing to be adventurous about food, provided nothing on my plate arrives with eyes or a pulse. Beverages carry a degree of ambiguity with which I am not comfortable. Seems counter-intuitive? Well, I already know to avoid ordering any goat brain entrée, or something I absolutely cannot consume. With a drink, we can often get fooled by an unfamiliar ingredient or combination, and then overlook it in the spirit of fitting in. This is how you find yourself on the wrong end of a $15 glass of Campari.

Stick with what you know, mostly. Try a foreign beer, if you have the gumption. An $8 mistake is easier to stomach, physically and philosophically. You are not going to impress your server no matter how accurately you pronounce "Carpano Punt e Mes." Everyone will be even less impressed when you make that face, as you realize just how awful vermouth is on its own.

Notable Potables

Carpano Punt e Mes
Vermouth with an orange slice

Rossini
Prosecco, strawberry purée

Via Napoli Ristorante e Pizzeria

It would not be Italy without a pizzeria, at least not in the pre-conditioned eyes of the average vacationing American. Via Napoli carries enough character and authenticity to warrant inclusion alongside the spectacular Tutto Ristorante and Wine Cellar. Via Napoli is a pizza place, in the same way Pirates of the Caribbean is a mere boat ride.

Many of the traditional dishes with which we are all familiar Via Napoli delivers with an artisan authenticity worthy of the Old World atmosphere. It's not just pizza. It's not simply spaghetti. What you get is a plate of heaven, to be enjoyed beneath the discriminating gaze of a wall of wood-fired ovens, or on a charmingly uncomfortable cast-iron table on the patio.

Wine lovers, you are in the right pavilion. Don't tell the French cast members I said so. Even the "pizza place" has an enviable wine list. There are no improper pairings. Pizza, pasta, even salad; I defy anyone to find a dish that doesn't go wonderfully with a glass of fermented wonder. The creative cocktails will delight those who are wined out.

Via Napoli also boasts a charming outdoor drinks cart. The hours are entirely unpredictable, and you can find all of these items elsewhere. When it's open, it's the easiest way to get an exceptional sorbet and beverage, without the wait or the pressure to procure an entire meal.

Notable Potables

Orangecello Cocktail
Orangecello liqueur, orange juice, pineapple juice, strawberry puree

Via Vesuvio
Blood orange vodka, Prosecco, raspberries

Rosa Regale
Banfi; sparkling Italian rosé

The American Adventure

Every pavilion ringing the World Showcase overflows with charm, character, and to these American eyes, authenticity. Mayan pyramids, tiny German villages, Italian architecture; the design and detail ignite sentiment and inspire longing, even if you have never been to their representative homeland.

Then we come to the American Adventure. It is charming. It possesses a wealth of character. But, as a native, I am curious whether it elicits a heightened level of wonder within our foreign visitors.

The massive colonial town hall is marvelous. The atmosphere surrounding the central theatre is glorious. Funnel cake and cheeseburgers adorn the bulk of what remains, and I wonder what that says about pure American culture.

I love funnel cake. I crave cheeseburgers far more than I ought to. Is that the best foot to put forward for guests from abroad? Every other pavilion exudes unmistakable and indispensable home-grown appeal. Doesn't the United States have a bit more to offer than deep-fat fryers and a bit of red brick?

This is not a criticism. I swell with pride coming into view of the Stars and Stripes. I do wish there was something more culturally outstanding than really good beer, and cardiovascularly questionable cuisine.

Specialty coffees are delicious. Those who have not had a jumbo turkey leg and Yuengling draft in combination have not lived. Does this all give first-time visitors from the eastern hemisphere the wrong impression? Worse, does this give off the precise impression, which is just not that spectacular? I haven't a discouraging word to say about the United States and my entire life within them. Does the American Adventure Pavilion instill pride among those who pass through it? I'm not always so sure.

In my world, IPA fixes everything. The American Adventure has a plethora. And, yes, every vendor and venue, down to the coin-press machine, sells Bud Light. It's a good way to remember where you are. The carts that offer gelato and margaritas throughout most of the park all display a higher frequency of light beer and blue Powerade.

Bloc & Hans

The American Adventure is bracketed by two delightful outdoor vending stands. One, Fife & Drum, is modeled in the signature red-brick style which dominates the pavilion. The other, Bloc & Hans, resembles a tiny Victorian manor, and is splendidly long on craft beer. Each provide a separate glimpse into the American culinary spirit. They should each serve baby-back ribs, in my opinion, though what they do offer is rather domestically outstanding.

There's not much in the way of food, but that's not an unforgivable offense when your menu is otherwise dominated by pure American craft brew. Okay, currently, one of the beers is from Sam Adams, and another is actually a hard cider. Each of these has a following, and with few ancillary food items to hold up the line, this is an excellent place to get beer no matter how few of the choices you favor.

There always seems to be at least one IPA, and it is always worth trying. On my last visit Honor Warrior IPA was featured. Honor Brewing is an excellent establishment, with an inspiring story and mission. Even if they aren't serving my favorite type of beer, which Walt Disney World just so happens to do, I will patronize Honor brands wherever and whenever I find them.

Notable Potables

Breckenridge Vanilla Porter
16 oz. draft

Honor Warrior IPA
16 oz. draft

McKnezie's Lazy Lemon Hard Cider

Fife & Drum Tavern

Three words: jumbo turkey leg. You have either had one from a Disney park, or your life is at least this one experience short of proper fulfillment. More of a project than a meal, until you have conquered one of these monstrosities, you may not know what it is like to truly accomplish something so worthwhile. I am not talking about finishing it. Most don't, and there's no shame in it. The goal is emerge from the task needing a bath, but with your clothes mostly intact. Do that—taste, feel, and smell jumbo turkey leg for the remainder of the day, and know what it means to live.

I like to pair my unwieldy turkey with Yuengling. Fife & Drum Tavern just so happens to have both. Hard soda, in several varieties, is also popular for pairing. I enjoy the taste of most of these beverages, though find this particular combination of very sweet and turkey-leg savory gives me heartburn.

Speaking of overindulgence and health risk, Fife & Drum offers both hard root beer and hard orange floats. When you finish your turkey leg, that is to say when you have gnawed on it to a point where it no longer looks like something safe to eat, if you haven't strayed too far down the walkway, grab dessert. Well, dessert and another drink.

Notable Potables

Frozen Red Stag Lemonade with Red Stag Black Cherry Bourbon

Hard Root Beer Float

Yuengling
16 oz. draft

Joffrey's Coffee & Tea Company

There are hundreds of carts, kiosks, and assorted outdoor vendors spread throughout the resort, where you may or may not be able to get an alcoholic beverage. Most of these places aren't named. Most don't appear on the guide maps. From day to day, many don't appear in the same location. Climate and crowd levels determine whether some of these vendors appear at all.

The American Adventure Joffrey's is a permanent fixture, and has a few grownup drinks on its regular menu. Joffrey's even gets into the festival spirit during Epcot's special events. It's surely blasphemy to patronize anything other than the incredible cultural outbuildings while visiting the Food & Wine and Flower & Garden Festivals. On a Saturday, though, when every other line spills over into neighboring pavilions, a frozen Joffrey's cocktail is a suitably inspired alternative.

Notable Potables

Frozen Strawberry-Lemon Sunset
Layered frozen strawberry and lemonade topped with Grey Goose vodka (Flower & Garden offering)

Shakin Jamaican
Joffrey's signature frozen cappuccino with Kahlua or Baileys topped with whipped cream

Liberty Inn

The ringleader of the American Adventure culinary circus. The lone American sit-down restaurant features two entrées (one of them is chicken nuggets) and it does not offer table service. I hate to keep harping on this pavilion. I love it, and my native country. I just wish it had something more spectacular to offer.

A fine steakhouse seems like an apt fit. If the steakhouse concept wasn't born in the United States, we have certainly, permanently adopted it. Sure, it would be difficult to compete with Tokyo Dining and Canada's Le Cellier, though is the point to compete or provide guests with a wholly enjoyable cultural experience? I don't even like steak. I understand it is delicious, though I don't relish a meal dominated by a huge hunk of meat (unless it's a jumbo turkey leg).

Again, the experience is what is important. Guests can come out of, say, Chefs de France, hungry because they ordered wrong, but will still benefit from the exposure to exquisite French dining. I love cheeseburgers. I live on salad with chicken in it. But, how does this benefit guests in terms of the American experience? What does it say about us? I love Epcot, and trust the creative minds involved almost implicitly. I've got to believe they can do better here.

Last time I visited, Liberty Inn was offering Sweet Potato Tortilla Chips and frozen Coke. This is a fine start on the road back.

Notable Potables

Yuengling
16 oz. draft

Frozen Coke with Buffalo Trace Bourbon Float

Japan

Separated by oceans and a few thousand years of disparate history, Japan is Italy's opposing book-end, bracketing the American Adventure. Mirroring the Italy Pavilion, somewhat, Japan is bristling with fine food and dramatic architecture. Theatrical performances, inspiring vistas, culture, charm, Nigori sake, and Azuki ice cream; this pavilion is everything you wish the American Adventure would be.

A word about drinking in Japan, the pavilion, and the country itself. Sake is very much like tequila, or bourbon, or any other culturally designated liquor with which most do not have regular exposure. It deserves your respect. If you are not aware how much of a certain spirit you can handle, it is wise to err on the side of moderation. When someone offers you a hot box of something you cannot pronounce or identify, the proper reaction is to refuse it.

Sake can be a wonderful glimpse into an alternate cultural tradition. More often it's like exceeding the prescribed dosage of a terrible and dangerous medication, including the predictable, disastrous results. Sake is known as rice wine. The only similarity to wine is in the headaches each precipitate. Please do try sake when visiting Epcot's Japan Pavilion. Please do not let anyone persuade you to engage in sake bombs, sake from a box, or the dreaded, "another round of sake."

Garden House

There are many wonderful drinking and dining venues in the Japan Pavilion. Several of them are quick-service. Each of these is wonderful, and won't cut unduly into your day. Garden House is an absolute bonus. It's essentially a specialized bar. It's even quicker than the quick-service alternatives, as it doesn't mess about with any of that complicated food.

Sake makes up roughly half the menu. With the proper will and supervision, drinking sake need not be hazardous. Without the proper appreciation for this seemingly innocuous liquid, you may not live to see Morocco. Nigori, unfiltered, is a personal favorite, in as much as I can claim to have a favorite sake.

There is also a full complement of what Westerners are to understand are Japan's most popular beers: Asahi, Kirin, and Sapporo. When I was in Japan, the country, everyone seemed rather partial to Budweiser. Interestingly enough, the Japan Pavilion is one of the few places in all of Walt Disney World where you won't find any Budweiser.

Notable Potables

Cucumber Cooler
Shochu with natural cucumber syrup

Nigori Unfiltered Sake

Sake Flight (3 2 oz. samples)

Kabuki Cafe

More ado about sake. Sake comes in various styles, flavors, and intensities. These cover a wide range of particular tastes, and it's completely reasonable to not know whether you even like any of them. Most sake that isn't dispensed in a steaming, wooden, coffee-cup-sized box is worth trying.

Kabuki Cafe has developed a concoction, Sake Mist, flavored with orange, coconut pineapple, and blackberry. I was skeptical, though I enjoy certain vodka blends in all three flavors. Turns out they each make an effective alcoholic shaved-ice flavoring, especially on a hot day. And, yes, all of them are better than the hot sake Kabuki offers, which you should avoid.

Kirin Frozen Draft is another interesting creation. It has been on the Kabuki menu for a few years now. I am surprised that we, the traveling public, are adventurous enough to sustain it. Yes, spätzle has long been available, just down the esplanade in Germany, and guests may feast upon soy curd right here in Japan. We seem a lot more willing to try an exotic dish we've never heard of, over a beer we have, served as a slurpee. This is something you ought to try, unless you dislike beer, or know you won't be able to stomach it in slush form. It's not bad. Sake Mist is better, though quite sweet.

Notable Potables

Sake Mist
Alcoholic shaved Ice available in blood orange, coconut pineapple, or blackberry

Kirin Frozen Draft
Japanese lager slurpee with foam on it (16 oz.)

Katsura Grill

For those who like the look of Kabuki Cafe, and are desirous of something a little more substantial, and perhaps a seat, Katsura is your next step up. If you could see around the pagoda a little better, Katsura would possess my favorite patio in the park. As it is, it's an exceptional place to sit, eat, drink, stay within your budget, and people watch, to a degree.

I once had Pork Ramen, from a noodle stand at the end of a concrete breakwater, in a Japanese hamlet called Ube. I sat by the harbor, eating my soup in some seasonably cold oceanic air, absorbing one of those truly transcendent foreign travel experiences.

No matter how often I travel abroad, I will never truly grasp these utterly surreal moments. Eating the world's best soup, in a town I wasn't aware of three hours prior, six thousand miles from my own home, on what is essentially someone else's driveway. No one knew me. No one knew or cared that I was there. Yet, it's a memory I will never shake, and one that contributes significantly to my overall sense of well-being.

The Tonkotsu from Katsura Grill takes me back there, every time. The taste. The smell. The scalding broth. Definitely not the climate. The next time I'm cold at Epcot will be the first time. I was warmer at five in the morning for a January runDisney event at Walt Disney World than I was at 3pm on that southern Japanese seaside. Still, every wonderful memory of that incredible, yet outwardly unspectacular moment comes flooding back. I also marvel, internally, how a $12 bowl of soup from Epcot is a bargain compared to what I paid for it from an essentially abandoned shack in Japan. You think Disney prices are steep? Go to the actual Japan sometime.

There are also a few beverages worth sampling. Beer drinkers thrill to the 20 oz. draft, while the frozen cocktail selection is as novel as it is wonderful. Try strawberry if you like it sweet. Green tea if less so. Both are tasty. Both could use an extra shot of alcohol.

Notable Potables

Kirin, Sapporo
20 oz. draft
Plum Wine

Mitsukoshi Department Store

While strolling the pavilion, looking for the attraction Japan should surely house, you ought to wander into this sizable market-style souvenir shop. Mitsukoshi has the charm and character of an authentic Japanese shopping experience, with far, far less of the hustle, bustle, and fish smell.

Check it out, even if you aren't of a mind to buy anything. The otherworldly gifts and delightful crew will help change your mind. That, or the sake stand in the back. They have beer you've never heard of. Get some. Cherish the novelty.

Notable Potables

Gingi Kogen Weizen
Japanese Hefeweisen-style beer (300 mL. bottle)
Filtered and Unfiltered Sake

Teppan Edo

Do you love your family? Of course you do. Can you spend all day, or week, with them at Disney World, then joyfully share a meal essentially sitting on top of one another, with everyone stealing from your plate? If not, I would beware Teppan Edo.

It's a blast, though Teppanyaki-style dining is not for everyone. A crowded theme park may not put one in the proper mood for such an experience. Spending an hour in the Soarin' standby line, listening to your kids complain about it, is not the best way to prepare for this festive, though intimate dining style.

As fed up as you may be with your own choir of angels, Teppanyaki carries the genuine possibility that you will be sharing your "table" with other guests. Having someone else's kids in your lap complaining about the heat, lines, and carnivorous insects offers a refreshing change. Just be sure you're prepared for it.

Preparation may come in the form of an exotic cocktail. Shochu, a Japanese barley-distilled spirit, doesn't deaden pain specifically, though is clinically proven to resuscitate frayed nerves. And by clinically, I mean after I had one, I didn't fret about the weather so much. And by one shochu, I mean two.

Notable Potables

Chu Hi
Japanese shochu, soda water, and orange, lemon, or grapefruit juice

Plum Wine
My mother like hers on the rocks. Try it.

Tokyo Dining

Exceptionally fine dining, Japanese style. I cannot claim the food is any better here than at Tutto Italia, or even right downstairs at Teppan Edo. The service and atmosphere, though, are out of this world. It's a little silly to hold the kindness and aptitude of any Disney cast member over any other. Still, I can comfortably brag on the Tokyo Dining crew.

In the United States, even at an authentic Japanese restaurant, when your server approaches the table to find you on your phone, having not even opened the menu, they will give you a telling, much deserved look. The Tokyo Dining cast member who caught me perpetrating this discourtesy became even more polite, if that's even possible. I tried to recover by quickly ordering a Japanese beer off the top of my head. Yeah, I picked one they don't carry.

Notable Potables

Green Tea Martini
Honey-infused matcha tea and vodka

Sake Mojito
Sake, shochu, Japanese shiso herb, and fresh mint

Morocco

Almost a forgotten pavilion, Morocco is beautiful and loaded with character. It doesn't have an attraction, or even a culturally enlightening theatrical exhibition. It does have two incredible restaurants, an exceptional and convenient quick-service counter, and a full bar. It also deserves some of your time.

Understandable, if you are passing through, and it's not mealtime, you may not think to stop. Hopefully, someone at a patio table will be drinking an enticingly bright tangerine concoction, and save you from making a poor and hasty decision.

Oasis Smoothie Stand

A rather convenient beer counter has been replaced with a stage for high energy, live Moroccan entertainment. The loss of any beer cart is felt the world over, but if you put something comparatively wonderful in its place, the effects are mitigated. Fortunately, there is a slushie and smoothie stand now right across from the stage that has everything the beer cart once had, and more.

The area simply screams out for a frozen beverage. If you aren't Drinking Around the World, take your pick. If you are engaged in the dubious over-consumption of Epcot alcohol, the stand sells Bud Light. Have one of those. Whichever direction you're heading, you've still got a long way to go.

Notable Potables

Habibi Daiquiri
Rum, strawberry purée, sweet and sour, orange blossom water

Sultan's Colada
Rum, pineapple, coconut juice, and almond liqueur

Restaurant Marrakesh

Come for the food, stay for the entertainment, drinks, ambience, and absolutely the food. You may be fortunate enough to live somewhere with a Moroccan restaurant nearby. It may even be the type of place that features authentic live entertainment. Unless Disney helped build it, and now runs it, it doesn't compare to this place.

Elaborate cultural dancing makes some people uneasy. I admit, I find someone else's bare stomach, in close proximity to my table while I am eating, a bit disquieting. Something about Restaurant Marrakesh lying within Walt Disney World assured me my wallet and reputation were not at risk, and I found the whole spectacle appropriate and enjoyable. Free-flowing Midori liqueur didn't hurt.

Notable Potables

Casablanca Sunset
Apricot brandy, orange juice, and cranberry juice, topped with peach schnapps

Marrakesh Express
Rum, orange juice, and pineapple juice, topped with dark rum

Spice Road Table

As much as I love it, the presence of a full bar inside a Disney park seems anathema. Perhaps it's the guilt I feel spending time on a Rose & Crown barstool, rather than pursuing attractions, photo opportunities, and sundry wholesome activities. The feeling is fleeting. It usually takes one sip of my first drink to remind me why I am in a Disney bar rather than slogging through a dispassionate standby line.

Describing every bar, restaurant, and footpath as charming is redundant. Within Disney's world of influence, though, it is entirely accurate. Disney puts as much thought, effort, and detail into its wholly adult pursuits as it does each family attraction. No, there aren't interactive trivia games to pass the time while waiting, though there is more than enough to see, and at which to marvel. Ordering a drink you've never heard of, that is Moroccan enough to satisfy the adventurous spirit that brought you here, is also worthwhile.

Notable Potables

Marbella Summer
Torres Brandy, Grand Gala Liqueur, strawberry purée, served frozen

Mediterranean Journey
Cointreau, peach vodka, and orange juice, topped with grenadine

Tangierine Café

Sometimes when you reach Morocco you aren't finished with the exotic glass of frozen splendor you acquired in France, or Japan, depending upon your direction of travel. You can either continue on through the Morocco Pavilion, or take a seat at the Tangierine Café, and enjoy the world for a while.

Tables inside are perfectly protected from the elements, except for a welcome breeze. The patio provides some Disney-patented people watching. Once you finish your beverage, understand you are not likely to find a similarly wonderful table without effort. So, hang out and get a Tangierine cocktail, or something similar, and perfect the fine art of leisure.

Notable Potables

Kasbah Coffee
Coffee, hazelnut liqueur, topped with whipped cream

Tangerine Daiquiri
Rum, Grand Marnier, and sweet and sour, served frozen

Casa Beer
12 oz. bottle

France

Food, wine, and beauty. All thoughts that come to mind when you consider France itself. The France Pavilion captures and delivers each. Why they can't do so with a dark or boat ride meandering through the area escapes me. Fine wine and Grand Marnier flow through the pavilion like the Seine, slightly mitigating the absence of an attraction. The recent success of *Beauty and the Beast* (2017) ought to inspire some Imagineering, no?

L'Artisan des Glaces

In *The Unofficial Disneyland Drinking Companion* (shameless plug), Award Wieners, a venue inside Disney California Adventure, which serves one single beer, drew some rather weighty criticism. At the risk of hypocrisy, L'Artisan des Glaces, too, only has one proper drink, yet garners our praise to a level that we almost named this chapter and my next cat after it.

Notable Potables

Ice Cream Martini
Two scoops of choice, with a shot of Grand Marnier, with vodka or rum and whipped cream

Chefs de France

When you fail to secure reservations for Monsieur Paul, or if you simply determine you don't want your kids leaving $40 entrées untouched, Chefs de France is a superb means of securing the fine French dining experience, without much of the wait and sticker shock.

The service, view, and menu are amazing. I discuss the slightly overblown reputation of dubious French table service, below, in my review of Monsieur Paul. Disney service is incredible, resort-wide. You are either a master of customer service, or you're looking for work somewhere else. Finding cast members more courteous and professional than those of the French Pavilion is a tall order. Chefs de France and Monsieur Paul are standard bearers.

For an excellent dining experience, without much of the financial premium, or dress code, Chefs has your table. It's also rather a nice place to enjoy an aperitif. Got a table by the window? Have a drink and stay awhile; if they aren't really busy.

Notable Potables

Kir Royal
Champagne Canard-Duchêne and black currant liqueur

St-Germain Cocktail
Sparkling wine, St-Germain Elderflower Liqueur and Perrier

Crepes des Chefs de France

With all of the glorious frozen and sparkling wonder that surrounds you in this portion of the park, not to mention the spectacular beer you just left behind in England, a Kronenbourg from a crêpe kiosk may not feel like an attractive alternative. During a peak period at Epcot, it may well be your only option.

Notable Potables

Kronenbourg
16 oz. draft

Les Halles Boulangerie & Patisserie

When Rose & Crown is full, when every inside table at Tangierine Café is occupied, Les Halles Boulangerie may be your only source for air-conditioned relief. It's not easy to pull yourself away from the esplanade, and past the beautiful fountain, though often the weather and the need for sanctuary demand it. Find solace, and a glass of authenticity, at this delightful, shaded snack shop.

Notable Potables

Bordeaux
Château De Richard

Mimosa
Champagne and orange juice

Les Vins des Chefs de France

Les Vins is enclosed, yes, but there's just nowhere to sit. Not to worry, as the most attractive item on the menu will shortly send you over to the Italy and Germany pavilions. "World Showcase Wine Walk" grants partons two 2 oz. servings of French, Italian, and German specialty wines. If it seems a little pricey, know that it ensures you guilt-free drinking at three pavilions. Perfect for those with family members who do not specifically share your enthusiasm for regular beverage stops.

Back out on the esplanade, Les Vins des Chefs de France quick-service kiosk shelters one of the best beverages on the planet. You may not think to look for it here, but do take notice of the unexpectedly long line at the mostly nondescript free-standing food-service counter. You may also not be expecting something so wonderful to come out of a slushie machine. It does, and it's still incredible. To be sure you completely love it, order "Le Geant." Same spectacular flavor with an extra shot of Grand Marnier.

Notable Potables

Orange Slush
Grand Marnier, rum and Grey Goose Orange, and orange Juice (single/double)

World Showcase Wine Walk
Two 2 oz. pours from France, Italy and Germany, with one complimentary reusable acrylic wine glass

Veuve Clicquot Brut Champagne

Monsieur Paul

There is an unsettled debate regarding Disney fine dining, over whether the food or service deserves the most praise. As a former cast member, and long-time slave for the service industry, I am always quick to credit an exceptional restaurant staff. Monsieur Paul's menu belongs in a museum, though the cast here could have been handpicked by Walt himself.

Americans, and Brits, frankly, give French servers a bad rap. Some of them, mainly Parisians, have earned it. I once had a waiter, in Paris, flat-out tell my party no, when we asked for water. Other cultures don't specifically cater to our every Western whim, and I try to remain sensitive to that when I travel. But, every other table in the cafe had a carafe of icy cold water on it. We asked for one, politely, I believe, and our waiter said no. It's one of the few French words I understand. It's also one of the few times I have been moved to walk out of a restaurant without ordering.

Deserved or otherwise, Monsieur Paul destroys the unkind stereotype. Part of the problem is that Americans often mistake professionalism for rudeness. The cast here is at once proficient and approachable. Disney isn't going to employ anyone who isn't friendly, and that includes historically stuffy French wait staff. Marvel at true masters of their craft, while not suffering intimidation. Buyer's remorse is a potential affliction, because Disney is also not going to shy away from making a few francs.

Notable Potables

Burgundy, Pinot Noir
Bourgogne Rouge, 2013 (glass/bottle)

Cordials
Grand Marnier, Armagnac, Courvoisier

Grand Marnier Flight
Three 1 oz. tastings: Cordon Rouge, 100th Anniversary, 150th Anniversary

United Kingdom

There are many who think drinking and Disney are incompatible. They should visit the United Kingdom Pavilion. Rather, since they sound fairly disagreeable, you should go there without them, and tip a pint to open mindedness.

One of the weightiest facets of the Disney magic is experienced the moment you enter a Disney park. For many it happens even sooner, simply driving onto the resort property and seeing the Disney sign. Guests are instantly transported to another world. Your memory of the outside starts to fade, and may do so completely, based upon the duration and intensity of your visit.

The United Kingdom Pavilion treats guests to a similarly concentrated, magical transformation. When you enter the Rose & Crown, you journey to a whole other world. The British pub replication is so complete, guests might forget they are in Epcot.

Rose & Crown Pub & Dining Room

Like everything Disney touches, Rose & Crown is a shiny re-creation of a real-world entity. Indeed, it's an improvement. It's clean. It's safe. The interior doesn't carry the odor of decades of spilt ale. The legs on the bar stools are all reliable and the same length. The commode works. You may not recognize everything on the menu, and what you order may not be entirely to your liking, but it will be cooked in a manner that won't kill you or end your vacation.

The Disney company is a victim of its own reputation and expertise. I note this every time I happen upon a Disney attraction, restaurant, shuttle, or information kiosk where the associated cast members are exceptional. When everyone is wonderful, it is difficult to find a standout, and we tend to take Disney customer service for granted. I marvel at guests who lament not receiving extra special treatment, not realizing that's exactly what they're getting. They don't realize it because everyone around them is also being so well treated. What they are truly seeking is something extra-extra special. Resources willing, they may get that as well. We do ourselves, and the cast, a disservice by insisting upon it.

La Cava del Tequila, Nine Dragons, Biergarten, Marrakesh; Epcot is bursting with inns, cantinas, boutiques, and restaurants shepherded by exceptionally personable, professional individuals. To say the crew at Rose & Crown stands out does not take away from other exemplary venues and cast members. Rose & Crown is indeed a rose within a field of roses, but with a diamond in it.

Rose & Crown is the type of place I wish I lived close enough to walk to. It is the vision I have for an ideal local hangout. I wouldn't want my local place to be so consistently popular, and I understand why Disney's pub doesn't have dart boards. Yeah, and I want foosball and happy hour and one of those slot-machine looking contraptions they have all over the UK, where no one ever wins.

If for nothing else, I come for Boddingtons. My first true pub ale came from a riverfront establishment in the London borough of Richmond upon Thames. It was a Boddingtons. I was in love.

Ask an American to drink a tepid, flat beer, with stuff potentially floating in it, and their response may not be positive. Let them discover the wonder of such a beverage, on a sylvan riverbank, where such beer was born, nurtured, and allowed to flourish, and they just might come around. I now know every bar, restaurant, and football pitch that sells Boddingtons within one-hundred kilometers of my house. I also know every time I travel to Walt Disney World, Rose & Crown is on my must-do list, and I will skip Soarin' to do it, if I have to.

Rose & Crown offers a full bar, and it's one of a few around the World Showcase where you aren't required to take/wait for a table. I tend to steer guests toward cultural and unfamiliar cocktails, except where the beer is this good. Also, if the featured drinks on the menu are any indication, I am not so sure about British cocktails. Something called the Leaping Leprechaun appears to resemble a Long Island Iced Tea, except it has Irish whiskey and melon liqueur in it. If you are Drinking Around the World, and include this, chances are, you won't make it to Canada or France.

Notable Potables

Leaping Leprechaun
Myer's Platinum Rum, Skyy Vodka, Jameson Irish Whiskey, melon liqueur, and sweet-and sour, topped with Sprite

Boddingtons English Pub Ale
Pint draft

Smithwick's Irish Ale
Pint draft

Black & Tan
Half Bass, half Guinness; pint draft

UK Beer Cart

The second time I ever visited the UK Beer Cart, I mistakenly got in the line for people putting their name in for a table at Rose & Crown. The two are side by side, and except for beer being dispensed from the one and not the other, they are difficult to tell apart. Fortunately the line wasn't long, and moved rather well. The down side: if you reach the front before figuring out your error, the charming kids with the accents will take your name, but will not pour you a beer.

Often, Rose & Crown Pub can get a little festive. Between general patrons, first-timers not knowing exactly what they want, and the cast being particularly social, you are unlikely to get a quick drink. This is part of the charm. If you're in there at all, plan to stay awhile, and be thankful.

When you don't have the inclination, or the time to spare, Rose & Crown is bracketed by this beer cart and a fish shop, either of which will have you sated and on your merry way. Neither has Boddingtons, thus I recommend you take the time to go inside, even if it looks like the World Cup is playing in the pub.

Those who must, may surely be happy with a Bass and a basket of crisps. Whenever I pass the Rose & Crown without stopping, I am smitten with a similar emotion as when I walk down Main Street, toward the Magic Kingdom exit, for the last time in a given visit. That feeling, for those who don't know, is called longing. It's a beautiful sensation, and no one elicits it like Disney.

Notable Potables

Bass Ale
Pint draft

Samuel Smith Pure-Brewed Organic Lager
Pint draft

Magners Pear Cider
Pint draft

Yorkshire County Fish Shop

Here we at least have the draw of glorious greasy fish. Still, the primary purpose of the fish shop and opposing beer cart are to provide guests with a beer, with which they may then queue up and wait to get served in the pub.

Note that two English ales, in quick succession, are not conducive to a philosophically wholesome Walt Disney World experience. I'm not saying don't do it, just take your time with the second one. It ought to be a Boddingtons, anyway. You'll want to savor it.

Notable Potables

Bass Ale
16 oz. draft

Harp Lager
16 oz. draft

Canada

There is so little known about Canada, by anyone not residing there, I am amazed it garnered enough interest to warrant its own pavilion. This is by no means a knock on this fine nation or its people. One of my favorite humans is Canadian. My sister married him. Considering the tourist dollars that go to Australia, Greece, Russia, and the like, I am a little surprised Canada made the cut. Mind you, given the beautiful representation, I am pleased. I also enjoy the beer.

Le Cellier Steakhouse

You don't come here to drink. Not specifically. Drinking Around the World binge teams ought to be politely turned away, for their own good. If you're having dinner in this amazing wine-cellar-styled venue, and don't have a drink, please surrender your table.

The most elegant restaurant underground, Le Cellier is also Epcot's most approachable fine diner. Grilled Sirloin is an option on the kids menu. Maine Lobster is available as an $18 enhancement. Do not be intimidated. Kids can opt for pasta, and the lobster is a mac & cheese dish. Have a beer, and relax, hey?

Notable Potables

Le Cellier Caesar
Iceberg Vodka, Clamato, Tabasco, Worcestershire, celery salt, pepper

Ottawa Apple
Crown Royal Maple Whiskey, apple infusion, cranberry juice

Le Fin Du Monde
16 oz. draft

Popcorn in Canada

Don't let the name, lacking in signature Disney creativity, fool ya. The charming cart has more than simply popcorn. It wouldn't appear in this guide, and would invite more scorn than Disney California Adventure's Award Wieners, if it didn't.

My brother-in-law is Canadian; sort of mentioned that above. Born and raised. He has lived all over North America's northern extremity. He likes popcorn, though can't tell me with confidence why Canadian popcorn rates highly enough to warrant its own booth. I love popcorn. I love Disney's conspicuously yellow popcorn, even here, where they choose to call it Canadian. I am disappointed, however, that this is not a snow cone kiosk. To be able to hold that particular stereotype over my brother-in-law's head would bring me simple pleasure.

They might have called this cart Beer in Canada. There are a few recognizable examples here. My bro assures me Labatt Blue and Moosehead are each arguably the Budweiser of Canadian brews. It fits, then, that they would be available, what with Bud Light adorning every other counter, kiosk, and ice-cream cart.

Notable Potables

Crown Royal Maple Whiskey

Le Fin Du Monde
16 oz. draft

Moosehead
16 oz. draft

Epcot's Drinking Around the World

Never participate in an actual Drinking Around the World competition. If you and a loved one want to sample a few of the exotic World Showcase offerings, please do. If you and some friends want to see how many different pavilions you can hit in one visit, and can stop before earnestly endangering anyone's health or reputation, consider that a day well spent. If, however, you are of a mind to slough from Mexico to Canada, the long way 'round, in a misguided attempt to consume a dozen disparate alcoholic beverages, at a family fun park, well, don't.

The rules are simple enough and should frighten even the most foolhardy away from ever attempting it. You may begin anywhere you like, though it is customary, given our predilection for moving clockwise, to start at Mexico. Each participant purchases and consumes a drink, then you move on to the next pavilion. This continues, theoretically, until you complete a full circuit of the World Showcase. That's eleven cocktails/beers in one visit, if you're counting just the pavilions. Throw in the ports and outposts, and you've got grounds for an intervention. In reality, most dubious guests stop when they get cut off, run out of money, or simply can't walk under their own power.

On paper, Drinking Around the World seems like a trough full of good times. Moving between the charmingly conceived and crafted Epcot pavilions, with fun-loving friends, sampling interesting, delicious, generally authentic concoctions. As the day progresses, your mood and interest in the activity climb to delightful heights. A refreshing Italian Bellini all but brings your party back from the Altenmünster disaster back in Germany.

Then, round about Morocco, even the most stalwart drinking bands will begin to succumb to the games undeniable rigors. This is where it will occur to you that you forgot to eat. This is also where you will have to admit the folly in not listening to that friend, the one to whom you were rather discourteous, who recommended you skip the Refreshment Cool Post. Yes, it serves alcohol, and who could resist a Frozen Elephant? But, it's not a pavilion, per se, and if you had any hope in this tragic pursuit, you would have passed on it.

If you make it to The American Adventure at all, you've got grit. You should probably also stop. I've alluded to this before, and shall again: you do not need to be drunk at Walt Disney World. No one in your group, proximity, or at the resort in general wants you to be. One drink, a couple foreign beers, a frozen something-or-other you can't pronounce, can appropriately add to a delightful day within the World Showcase. Eleven, or more, alcoholic beverages within the span of one visit to Epcot is, quite literally, a recipe for disaster.

If I haven't convinced you, then here's how to go Drinking Around the World:

Grab a free Epcot guidemap. Pick your favorite, or a random, or just the most convenient World Showcase pavilion. Also, probably should have said this first, only Drink Around the World with people you implicitly trust. Do not engage in this activity with anyone enthusiastic or insane enough to try to do it officially, all the way through, in one trip. Equally important, do not do it with anyone negligent enough to let you attempt it in one shot. If your friends and loved ones truly care about you, they will join you in breaking up the endeavor into three or four well-tempered, pleasantly memorable segments.

If you start in Mexico, and you really should, try your luck at the crowd-favorite La Cava del Tequila lounge. There will be a crowd, there may even be a line. If you have the patience, the bounty and service inside are worth any wait.

After committing to do it responsibly, the best way to approach Drinking Around the World is to try drinks you've never had, and perhaps have never even heard of. Beginning with a tequila libation seems to betray our advice, though no one is telling you to firehose it. The offerings at La Cava del Tequila are so inherently wonderful, it pains me to think of anyone consuming a Maelstrom as their fifth or sixth drink.

It'll be difficult to enjoy, or even rightly taste it. I am also tired of having my relaxation disrupted by groups of drunks descending upon one of my favorite hangouts as their ninth stop on their road trip to oblivion.

Wherever you tour begins, there are two equally popular avenues of pursuit. One camp prefers to enjoy their drinks in the pavilion, cantina, or pub in which they are purchased. The alternative is to take your drink to go. Both approaches have their advantages and pitfalls. In the first case, you get to spend quality time in each pavilion, and it is rather easy to plot your next stop. When finished, if still able to walk, make your way to the next pavilion along your route, and repeat. Depending upon your tolerance, this option limits the amount of park you will see, or remember.

The on-the-go alternative is better for exploring the park, unless you combine it with the stop-at-the-next-pavilion approach. These are the groups that are determined to ruin their own day, and they are rather easy to spot. I applaud the mindful who make the long, laborious trek between nations with a delicious beverage in tow. It falls apart among those who arrive at the next pavilion with three-quarters of their drink left, then insist upon slamming it.

This is a dubious contest at best. Those who incorporate a speed element are doomed to an ignoble, likely spectacular failure. There is no shame in showing up at Norway with a mostly unfinished margarita, or Green Tea Slush, depending upon which direction you favor. Slow down. Enjoy your drink, the park, and the potential for the day spread out before you. If your friends are hustling into Akershus without you, remember, perhaps you've latched onto the wrong crew for this.

The purists go pavilion to pavilion, but there are no hard-and-fast rules. You don't have to go in order. You don't even have to maintain the same direction the entire time. Such changes complicate the logistics, though that can only serve to shorten the game for you, which is not necessarily negative. If you can't keep track of where you've been, you need to stop anyway.

If you are determined to Drink Around the World, and want to make the most of the experience; positive cultural appropriation is the name of the game. Do not simply have a beer at every pavilion. Such behavior is lazy, and violates the spirit of the adventure, almost as severely as getting drunk while doing it. Yes, have beer in England, Germany, and the American Adventure. Everywhere else boasts some type of unfamiliar authentic libation, and this is your prime opportunity to try them.

The Italy Pavilion serves beer. So does Japan, Canada, Norway, Morocco, and France. Mediterranean beer, as an example, is absolutely worth your patronage. Epcot may represent your best and only time to try it. Have one when you go to dinner at Spice Road Table. As part of your international tour, wander out of your comfort zone a little. Favor a specialty drink. You needn't pay $12 for something you aren't likely to enjoy. I like trying drinks I've never heard of, but I remain aware of ingredients. Ouzo is not for everyone. Jägermeister shouldn't be available at all. But there is a wide margin between paint thinner and barley water where guests can enjoy themselves quite thoroughly. But if your goal is to drink twelve beers, maybe go bowling.

Showcase Plaza

While Drinking Around the World, if you find yourself between the Promenade Refreshments and the Refreshment Port, you essentially have three choices: (1) skip them both, (2) quit, (3) visit them both, and use the questionable move to justify quitting.

When not Drinking Around the World, Showcase Plaza refreshment options are delightful and accessible, most of the time. While guests fill every Rose & Crown barstool, and render La Cava del Tequila untenable, Showcase Plaza walk-up counters often remain relatively unobstructed. At peak periods, and especially during the Food & Wine Festival, you can't even get to a drinking fountain in Epcot. In general, probably because they aren't attached to one of the international pavilions, and thus no clever, compelling theme, you can usually count on these venues for a quick bite and a beer.

Promenade Refreshments

Promenade serves Yuengling, at least for now. I prefer my American lager from the American Adventure, but I will bet you can finish any drink you get from Promenade Refreshments before you get all the way around to there. If not, you either walk too fast, or drink too slow. Neither serves you well at Epcot.

Notable Potables

Cigar City Jai Alai IPA
16 oz. draft

Sea Dog Sunfish
16 oz. draft

Refreshment Port

Refreshment Port has a surprising beverage list for being unattached and essentially out of the way. True, it's only three cocktails and one beer, so not overwhelming, but one of those cocktails is an Absolut Bloody Mary with blue cheese-stuffed olives. I would sit through the still mangled Journey into Imagination twice to get one of those.

The concoction is called the Stow Away Mary, and it's obnoxious. Who puts chicken nuggets in a drink? Once you pair down the cumbersome garnish, though, you are left with an extraordinary beverage, with which you could get all the way to the BoardWalk, if they'd let you leave Epcot with it (they won't).

Notable Potables

Stow Away Mary
Classic Bloody Mary with Absolut Vodka garnished with blue cheese-stuffed olives, celery, and tomato, topped with fried chicken breast nuggets

Dragon Berry Refresher
Featuring Bacardi Dragon Berry Rum

Godiva Hot Cocoa
Hot cocoa with Godiva Liqueur

Bud Light
16 oz. draft

Future World

Drinking around Future World does not hold near the same allure as the cultural World Showcase alternative. Don't let that stop you from seeking out and enjoying adult refreshment in the more modern end of the park. There are delicious, creative options everywhere. Guests needn't settle for Bud Light at an outdoor vendor simply because it's so readily available. Peruse a few menus. When your patronage ensures specialty beer and cocktails will be available for future generations, they will surely thank you in their own way, with underwhelming dispassion.

Coral Reef Restaurant
The Seas with Nemo & Friends

A hypnotically nautical wonder. One entire wall of the dining room is an aquarium. I have trouble fine dining in Epcot and not doing it in one of the many incredible international pavilions. I need to get over that. Coral Reef is an experience as much as a meal.

The service is predictably wonderful, though desperately underappreciated. Not surprising, since the cast members aren't swimming in the wall. There are live sharks, though. Hard to compete with that.

Not sure if it's ironic or appropriate that this is a seafood restaurant. At any rate, Reef Amber beer pairs wonderfully with char-broiled octopus.

Notable Potables

The Abyss
Skyy Vodka, Bacardi Superior Rum, blue curaçao, pineapple juice

Coral 'Rita
A margarita with Patrón Añejo Tequila and Cointreau

Piña CoLAVA
Bacardi Raspberry Rum blended with piña colada mix and raspberry purée

Reef Amber
22 oz. draft

Electric Umbrella
Innoventions East

Umbrella has about as much indoor seating as you are going to find in a Walt Disney World quick-service restaurant. There is a delightful patio as well, nicely positioned for a consistent breeze, though it's still too hot out there, most of the time.

I remember getting french fries from here when I was a kid, then wandering into Innoventions and being considerate enough not to gum up the touch screens with my greasy fingers. It's a close contest, but I miss the old Innoventions almost as much as the Imagination Pavilion that I once adored.

My point in bringing it up is that I don't know whether Electric Umbrella, or whatever it was called way back when, served cocktails. That would have been quite an extra layer of wonderful, if you could construct touch-screen roller coasters, solve traffic issues, and load baggage over margaritas.

Walking Innoventions now, with a beer in tow, it's impossible not to miss the Atari-level technology, the trivia robot, and a time when guiding a mouse through a maze with your own voice was really, truly amazing.

Notable Potables
Heineken
16 oz. draft
Piña Colada
Strawberry Margarita

Fountain View
Innoventions West

It's a Starbucks. How hard is it to bring in a couple bottles of Baileys? Another missed opportunity, if you ask me (see Magic Kingdom, Aloha Isle).

The Garden Grill
The Land

Get a Raspberry Mimosa, then remember to keep it away from your children. It looks exactly like the kind of drink they would love, and there is all kinds of distraction within Garden Grill. It would be easy to lose track of something like this.

I try to caution anyone drinking at a Disney character breakfast, though I am more concerned about adults who do not. I love the characters. I even love the chaos they create in a restaurant specifically designed for this purpose. I'm not about to spend the entire duration of a meal in this culinary tornado without the pacifying influence of a Disney Bloody Mary.

I marvel at (question) the mental wherewithal of those who purposely eat here and don't drink. Worse are those downstairs in the Soarin' standby queue, who aren't drinking. I know Disney discourages bringing alcohol into certain areas of the parks. If you try to get in line with a Stow Away Mary, or bottle of wine, you are going to attract the wrong kind of attention. That Soarin' line does anything but soar, though. I would pay Garden Grill servers in gold to run down a round of Citrus Freezes every twenty minutes.

Notable Potables

Citrus Freeze
Florida Cane "Orlando Orange" Vodka, peach schnapps, and mango purée

Raspberry or Orange Mimosa
Breakfast only

Orlando Brewing I-4 IPA
12 oz. bottle

Yuengling
12 oz. bottle

The Land Cart

The Land
One of the few outdoor vending carts to make the online map, this cart is a remarkable, mostly hidden gem for beer drinkers during peak days, hours, and festivals. It can draw a crowd. This most often happens when a guest gets the fruit-and-cheese plate, then eats it in plain view of other guests. When it occurs to visitors you can get something so convenient and healthy, they flock to it. I did. I got the hummus pretzel. Then I sat with it in my lap, staring at what's left of the Imagination Pavilion, with deep longing.

Notable Potables

Sea Dog Sunfish
16 oz. draft

Yuengling
16 oz. draft

Sunshine Seasons
The Land

Grab-and-go grub, yet the fare is good. It might also have to do with ample seating and air conditioning. You will surely get a quicker drink from The Land Cart, out front. The looping walk through The Land Pavilion is not the most efficient use of your steps. On a hot day, there are many of them, so even an unnecessary walk inside is welcome.

The selection is food-court typical. So, yeah, Bud Light, Yuengling, Corona, and a couple varieties of wine. Completely serviceable if you're in the dining room having fish tacos. But unless you have come in to get out of the heat, to use the restroom, or have decided to bail out of the ridiculous Soarin' line, several better options await.

Notable Potables

Yuengling
16 oz. can

Angry Orchard Crisp Hard Apple Cider
16 oz. can

Taste Track
Test Track

An incredible treat, especially on predictably hot and humid Florida afternoons. If there weren't many preferable frozen delicacies waiting in Mexico, China, Japan, Morocco, and France, to name a few, just steps away, I might drink hard floats from here all day.

There can be a crowd here, on occasion. Walt Disney World guests really like ice cream, and most of them aren't sympathetic to how desperately you want root beer with booze in it. It's worth the wait, when this is what you want. Plus, it's far less waiting than you will ever do at La Cava del Tequila.

Notable Potables

Henry's Hard Orange Float with Vanilla Ice Cream

Not Your Father's Hard Root Beer Float with Vanilla Ice Cream

Test Track Cool Wash

Test Track

Another hidden gem, in the shadow of Test Track. There are some incomparable margaritas and fruit slushies waiting for you all around the World Showcase, so I wouldn't wear out my gift cards here. It is a long walk to France, and you may never get there on certain Saturdays. Maybe take a blue frozen drink to go and see how many people ask, "Where did you get that?" as you make your way around the lagoon.

Notable Potables

Frozen Beverages
Your choice of Grey Goose, Jack Daniel's, or Captain Morgan Original Spiced Rum

CHAPTER TWO

Disney's Hollywood Studios

Is anyone still lamenting the removal of Mickey's sorcerer hat? If so, they likely haven't seen the scintillating Star Wars Spectacular. It's a lesson in trusting Disney's decision making. Yes, those were Disney minds that conceived Alien Escape, and Disney decisions led to the current state of Epcot's Imagination Pavilion. Yet, even when it is at the expense of something beloved, most often the results are positive.

Disney's Hollywood Studios continues to undergo a major overhaul. The removal of the Osborne Family Lights is, at the moment, difficult to process or forgive. Faith, trust, and pixie dust, so the saying goes. With that, and a little patience, I think we're going to witness another profoundly positive evolution.

I appreciate the rising frequency of wholly creative specialty drinks, and lounges in which to enjoy them. The Hollywood Brown Derby, Tune-In, heck, even the Pretzel Palooza stand has multiple adult beverage options, and the ice cream vendors sell SweetWater Pale Ale. Epcot will long be the primary draw for cultural culinary enthusiasts and drinking teams, but Disney's Hollywood Studios is making significant progress in the proper direction. The development of Star Wars- and Pixar-dedicated lands can only elevate the surrounding creativity.

50's Prime Time Café
Echo Lake

The menu here is as dated as the decor, and that's what makes it so wonderful. When was the last time you had succotash?

I wouldn't blame you for not ordering it. It's just heartwarming, if stomach wrenching, to see it at a restaurant.

Most of the featured drinks come from Disney's well-established specialty drinks menu. That particular menu could use some serious updating, though it fits perfectly with 50's Prime Time Café's nostalgic aura.

I cannot recommend ordering any of these particular cocktails. It is still not a knock on the menu. It's just that Echo Lake is now swimming with incredible adult beverages. Mere steps outside, Min and Bill's and Oasis Canteen offer adult drinks far and above what you would expect to find at an unattached snack shack, even one designed by Disney. This doesn't do diners much good within Prime Time Café. But, get this: if you want a drink with your meal here, I would even suggest having a Bud Light. I know, right?

The Magical Star Cocktail is a tiny slice of Disney history. If having one preempts you from having something, let's be honest, that you will actually enjoy, then even the multi-colored souvenir glow cube isn't worth it.

Notable Potables

Grandma's Picnic Punch
Skyy Vodka, peach schnapps, crème de cassis, light lemonade, and pineapple juice

Cigar City Jai Alai IPA
16 oz. draft

ABC Commissary
Commissary Land

When choosing a place to eat at a Disney park, several factors weigh on the decision. Well, they ought to. Seating, shade, climate control, peak traffic patterns, IPA; all elements that should weigh on your decision. Put thought into it, or join those people, at which you presently marvel, who stand in ridiculous food lines, only to crowd around a trash can, eating a hamburger in the sun.

From the outside, or on the map, the ABC Commissary may not look like much. It may not have the charm of the 50's Café, or the Sci-Fi Dine-In next door. It also won't have the wait those places have. It does have air conditioning. It has plenty of comfortable, if not creatively inspired seating. It has ribs. It has a couple of really good salads. It serves beer and wine.

You aren't going to have your favorite meal here, unless posters of past and present ABC television shows truly ignites your pilot light. You also aren't going to have to sacrifice a FastPass+, or significant slice of your budget or itinerary.

Notable Potables

Yuengling
16 oz. draft

Robert Mondavi Wine

Anaheim Produce
Sunset Boulevard

Disney delights in pleasant surprises. Whether it's a Tiki room full of talking birds, the First Order muscling you off Hollywood Boulevard, life-like plant life on stilts on Discovery Island, or your favorite beer at an obscure fruit stand, unexpected thrills and hidden details await at every turn.

Every park and property is a testament to going outside your comfort zone. If you always ride the same rides, eat at the same restaurants, travel the same path, you are doing yourself, and Disney, a disservice. Everything you do is inherently wonderful. Still, explore a little.

Disney's Hollywood Studios is ripe with unanticipated opportunity. Along with an exceptional Italian Restaurant in Muppet Courtyard, and a delicious Kahlua Milkshake served out of a dockside dinosaur, you may find your favorite local beer at a fruit stand on Sunset Boulevard.

Anaheim Produce isn't long on food of any kind. The hook here is craft beer and frozen cocktails. The selection seems to rotate regularly. If you like a little flavor behind your brew, if Kona or Magic Hat are there when you are, get it. The shock shouldn't be extreme if they have neither. The replacements are likely to be similar and interesting.

Notable Potables

Kona's Longboard Island Lager
16 oz. draft

Magic Hat #9 Not Quite Pale Ale
16 oz. draft

Schöffhoffer Pink Grapefruit Hefeweizen
16 oz. can

Angry Orchard Crisp Apple Hard Cider
16 oz. can

Frozen Golden Margarita

Backlot Express
Echo Lake

Star Wars-themed eatery. I have yet to convince the otherwise accommodating Backlot cast members to pour me a Yuengling in the Chewbacca Souvenir Stein. The primary issue is probably that I don't offer to pay the extra $12 to get it.

I have a disturbing memory of being here as a kid. I don't know if the Backlot Express existed back then, though there was a drinking fountain that fire-hosed water into my face. Through twenty years of landscape and architectural renovations, the drinking fountain is still here. And it got me again.

Notable Potables

After Burner
Angry Orchard Crisp Hard Cider and Fireball Cinnamon Whisky

Yuengling
16 oz. draft

Frozen Golden Margarita

Catalina Eddie's
Sunset Boulevard

Another of the Disney-fashioned farmer's market stands off Sunset Boulevard. Each is a bounty of quality and not-super-expensive consumables, with variety and often very little waiting. As the Brown Derby, Sci-Fi, and Backlot Express fill to capacity, the assorted Sunset Boulevard quick-service counters virtually beckon. Each has its own personality and particular draw. What they don't have are waiting lists and $50 filet.

Eddie's doesn't have Anaheim Produce's craft beer selection. It does have Sierra Nevada, at least for now, and it does have pizza. There are several splendid food offerings at Hollywood Studios. If you are keen on real Italian, head over to Muppet Courtyard. For something a little simpler, with less of a walk, and still a really good beer, stay here.

Notable Potables

Beso Del Sol Sangria

Sierra Nevada Pale Ale
16 oz. draft

Fairfax Fare
Sunset Boulevard

Very similar to Catalina Eddie's, with a slight southwestern bent. You will find yourself here when one of your children won't eat pizza, or chicken, or anything else everyone else has agreed to. Do not despair. The line is quick, and the beer is good.

Notable Potables

Sierra Nevada Pale Ale
16 oz. draft

Yuengling
16 oz. draft

The Hollywood Brown Derby Restaurant and Lounge
Hollywood Boulevard

The crown jewel of Hollywood Studios dining, which is saying something, as the park arguably rivals Epcot for creative kitchens and cuisine. Derby's old-school styling possesses an almost cult-like allure, rendering this, and Disney California Adventure's Carthay Circle, popular beyond practicality. I don't recommend waiting unduly for a table in this restaurant. To experience the Derby, though, that is often your only option, and it's just as often not available either.

Occasionally the weather is such that an outside table will be available, though it can be difficult to get into the martini-sipping spirit in either the rain or the blistering sunshine. Bordering on the impossible, if you can get a lounge table in the early evening, you will be counted among the blessed. If you have the foresight and alcohol tolerance to hang out until the Star Wars Galactic Spectacular, count yourself among the brilliant. The angle does not provide ideal viewing, and you will have to stand up when people park right in front of you. Since getting a prime viewing spot in the middle of Hollywood Boulevard requires waiting even longer than you did for a Derby table (and those spots are without cocktail service), you are much better off, and have enviably well-tuned priorities.

Notable Potables
Derby Margarita
Sauza Commemorativo Tequila, Cointreau, and sweet and sour, topped off with Grand Marnier (ask for a splash of Sprite or orange juice, or both, in place of sweet and sour)

Dorma Nesmond Martini
Ketel One Citroen, pomegranate liqueur, and cranberry juice

The Fabulous Mariness
Absolut Pears Vodka, Patrón Silver, lime juice, muddled strawberries, and cilantro

Hollywood Scoops
Sunset Boulevard
I weep for the overwrought parents who deny ice cream to their children, not realizing Hollywood Scoops serves a high-octane root beer float. These drinks are a bit sweet and cream heavy. Securing that well-imbibed feeling through such can cause unwanted ancillary physical issues. That's a good thing, really, and saves us from ourselves. Probably the only thing more disreputable than simply being drunk at a Disney park is to do so abusing ice cream drinks.

Notable Potables
Coney Island Hard Root Beer Float with Vanilla Ice Cream

Hollywood & Vine
Echo Lake

Character dining, so you better believe they serve alcohol. I assumed from the description, since this character buffet features Disney Junior celebrities rather than more mainstream classic characters, that Hollywood & Vine would have a different vibe. I was mistaken, and should know better than to underestimate Disney, in any regard. The kids are just as enthusiastic, the characters are every bit as professional, and the spectacle, for those who come to be entertained, is sensational.

Even though Goofy and Elsa aren't going to parade through the dining room, the whole thing is every bit as well attended, and loud. Find solace in the presence of the Disney specialty cocktails menu, then locate, order, and enjoy your favorite. Don't be afraid to order a second beverage; it gives one all the more reason to tip the poor kid removing the ceaseless rotation of dirty dishes from your table.

Notable Potables

Captain's Rum Runner
Captain Morgan Original Spiced Rum, blackberry brandy, créme de banana, and tropical juices, topped with a float of Myers's Original Dark Rum

Magical Star Cocktail
X-Fusion Organic Mango and passion fruit liqueur, Parrot Bay Coconut Rum, pineapple juice, and a souvenir multi-colored glow cube

KRNR The Rock Station
Sunset Boulevard

This glorified food truck is located next to Rock 'n' Roller Coaster. It might well be called the Tailgate Party, as the only food offering is a chili cheese dog, and every drink features either Jack Daniel's or Budweiser. I haven't a particular issue with either, though KRNR is also in the vicinity of Tower of Terror. Don't eat here and sit behind me on the neighboring attractions, please.

Notable Potables

Frozen Lemonade Cooler
Comes with a shot of Bacardi Superior Rum, Jack Daniel's Tennessee Whiskey, or Three Olives Cherry Vodka

Jack and Coke

Mama Melrose's Ristorante Italiano
Muppet Courtyard

Were PizzeRizzo not so close, convenient, and, let's be honest, cheap (relatively), I would come to Mama Melrose's every visit. A native southern Californian, I am predisposed to Mexican food. Still, I spent enough mealtimes in suitably authentic Italian restaurants to develop an appreciation for them. Mama Melrose's takes me back.

I don't know if someone has to order seafood cioppino for the foyer to smell like heaven and bouillabaisse. What I do know is everything in this corner of the park triggers the smell receptors in my brain to release the kind and quantity of endorphins that make me really happy. That's a thing, right?

There are far too few places upon this earth that carry and serve Van Gogh Vodka. Double Espresso Martinis are hard to find, even among places that do. It has such a pungent coffee presence, it's surprising the Double Espresso Martini recipe also calls for Kamora. Baileys helps offset the taste, though as the third alcohol in this one drink, it will also affect your balance. Have one, it's well worth the risk.

Drink Van Gogh Vodka wherever you find it. Demand it where you don't.

Notable Potables

Bellini Cocktail
A refreshing combination of sparkling wine, white peach, and raspberry

Double Espresso Martini
Van Gogh Double Espresso Vodka, Kamora Coffee Liqueur, Baileys Irish Cream, and half & half

Tiramisú Martini
Stoli Vanil Vodka, Kamora Coffee Liqueur, and vanilla ice cream in a chocolate-drizzled glass

Min and Bill's Dockside Diner
Echo Lake

During my last Walt Disney World trip, I was determined to settle a critical, long-standing issue: is a Kahlúa and Cream Milkshake better with chocolate or vanilla ice cream? I love them both, though have never had them back-to-back on the same visit. I know myself well enough to realize that I am entirely partial to whichever favored drink I'm having, at any given time. In the case of the milkshake, the one I like best is the one in my hands and gullet.

Choosing between two similarly wonderful beverages, for someone with my refined, yet capricious tastes, requires sampling them almost simultaneously. No, I do not intend to purchase $24 worth of milkshake all at once, though it might be what is necessary to reach a reliable conclusion. Despite my adoration for this delicious drink, I'm not sure I'm willing to sacrifice the block of time this would necessitate.

Echo Lake is a delightful place to sit, people watch, and drink multiple blended cocktails. These drinks are gloriously large, and too good to hoard. If you suffer brain freeze drinking something this delicious, you're doing it wrong. Two milkshakes will eat up a considerable amount of your park time. The solution: get the chocolate, go ride a ride or see a show, then come back for the vanilla.

The reason I truly don't know which flavor milkshake I like best is because the Oasis Canteen, just around the lake, sells Dreamsicle and Stoli Vanilla root beer and floats. Milkshakes and floats cloud the nervous and digestive system, and I can't resist either. Wait until you hear the ordeal surrounding choosing between those two (see below).

Notable Potables

Kahlúa and Cream Milkshake
Comes with a shot of Baileys Irish Cream (choice of chocolate or vanilla)

Robert Mondavi Woodbridge Chardonnay, Cabernet

Oasis Canteen
Echo Lake

The Stoli Vanilla with Root Beer vs. Dreamsicle Float debate makes the milkshake dilemma (above) seem as pointless as deciding which end of a straw to use. Two incredible tastes taken straight out of my childhood, it is amazing to find them at an outdoor vendor, in a Disney park, in such similar form.

Root beer helps cut the vanilla-on-vanilla sweetness. This is the best root beer float you will ever have. I say that independently of the euphoric alcoholic after-effect. On the other hand, the minds behind this have perfectly reproduced the Dreamsicle flavor. Dreamsicles are still widely available; I just never get them. Having access to one at Disney World, with a quality Stoli product mixed in, is more than I can resist.

As for which float is better, that will depend upon your particular taste, mood, and, if you're like me, which one you most recently ordered. What I know for certain is that I like both better than the specialty drinks on the 50's Prime Time Café menu. Thus, while enjoying a meal within Disney's Hollywood Studios, don't squander your cocktail capacity and rations on inferior beverages. Of course, you may have a drink at lunch, then another when you reach Oasis, though it's sure to affect your Midway Mania abilities.

Notable Potables
Dreamsicle Float with Stoli Vanil Vodka
Root Beer Float with Stoli Vanil Vodka

PizzeRizzo
Muppet Courtyard

I went on at some length earlier, propping up the ABC Commissary. I stand by what I wrote: it's a convenient, quick, and comfortable place to grab a meal and glass of something. You can find all those elements at a number of other venues, and most of them are more charmingly conceived and presented. PizzeRizzo is one of the best. In this park, it's my favorite.

I can't swear it's not coming exclusively from Mama Melrose's next door, but the authentic Italian restaurant smell hanging over Muppet Courtyard is enough to bring and keep me there. As an aside, the new Star Wars addition is going to be right behind the courtyard. I am curious how they are going to tie in the undeniable garlic-bread scent. It's a truly delicious olfactory presence, but it's going to take some Spielberg-like brilliance to make it fit seamlessly into the galactic landscape. A Jar Jar breadsticks stand, perhaps?

With no idea how a Wildberry-Basil Limoncello Lemonade relates to the Muppets, it is available at PizzeRizzo, for whatever reason, and I love it. Once upon a time I could not drink anything sweeter than a margarita, and even those were only tolerable when made with enthusiasm (mucho tequila). Back then I wouldn't wash my socks in a wildberry lemonade.

My tastes have since evolved, to my benefit. If you avoid a food or beverage because it sounds bad, you might be doing yourself a disservice. I am not suggesting you give in to escargot or kombucha, or similar atrocities. There are certain substances that are just inherently not meant to be in your mouth, and I don't fault anyone's preconceptions regarding them. But every so often, give something you haven't had in a while a try. It just might surprise you.

For me, the Wildberry-Basil Limoncello Lemonade is one such delightful revelation. Just enough basil to appease the willful, though be wary, it's still pretty sweet. It's also not terribly strong. It pairs with the PizzeRizzo meatball sub like nothing else for which I've developed a craving. I know the setting and atmosphere play a significant role. Call it a comfort meal, but I eat here, and I order this, even when I'm not hungry.

Notable Potables
Woodbridge
Robert Mondavi Cabernet Sauvignon, Chardonnay
Wildberry-Basil Limoncello Lemonade

Rosie's All-American Café
Sunset Boulevard

Another of the serviceable, convenient dining counters on Sunset Boulevard, Rosie's is a hidden food-and-beverage blessing. Have you ever had a fried green tomato sandwich? Coming from a relatively obscure snack stand, in essentially a Disney alley, this particular fried green tomato sandwich is spectacular. Two significant components are jalapeño and ciabatta bread. Make sure you like both before ordering.

Smirnoff gets a bit of a bad rap, mostly for being so reasonable. When you are mixing liquor and juice, you really don't need a premium-priced product. Smirnoff Raspberry Lemonade is as unexpected and pleasantly surprising as the ciabatta, jalapeño, fried tomato sandwich from the same window. Don't celebrate your anniversary here, or anything. Unless you met here originally. That would be adorable.

Notable Potables

Captain Morgan Fruit Punch Cocktail
Smirnoff Raspberry Vodka Lemonade
Sierra Nevada Pale Ale
16 oz. draft

Sci-Fi Dine-In Theater Restaurant
Commissary Lane

When Disney Imagineers are given sufficient financial and creative leeway, magic happens. Be Our Guest and Tiffins are contemporary examples of Disney's finest, most charming restaurants. For a glimpse of the vintage character spectacle, roll into Sci-Fi Dine-In Theater Restaurant.

You don't have to be an old Twilight Zone or monster movie fanatic to appreciate this classic creation. This is authentic Disney creativity on display. The food, service, and atmosphere are more than worth the potential wait. I have always had a soft spot for Pirates of the Caribbean, Biergarten Restaurant, the Mexico Pavilion, and Disneyland's Blue Bayou, where you become immersed in the nighttime scene, and can completely forget it is still day outside. Sci-Fi Dine-In is one such place, and if nothing else, it's air conditioned.

Notable Potables

Long Island Lunar Tea
Bacardi Superior Rum, Tito's Handmade Vodka, Hendrick's Gin, Cointreau, and sweet and sour, with a splash of Coke

Orbiting Oreos
Oreo Shake mixed with Godiva Chocolate Liqueur and a souvenir glow cube

Napa Smith Brewery Hopageddon IPA
16 oz. draft

Ticket Central
Hollywood Boulevard

At the corner of Hollywood Boulevard and Sunset, an unobtrusive snack cart patiently saves the lives of savvy beer drinkers. You may not know it by name, and it's not on the map. There's usually a crowd around, though most of it is engaged in trying to figure out the FastPass+ machines.

Depending upon the time of day, and associated climate conditions, this unheralded outdoor vendor may have exactly what you need. First of all, it currently sells SweetWater 420, an exceptional representation of the pale ale category; there are times, albeit only a few, when I prefer this option to an IPA. When I know I am headed over to face tedious lines for sugar-laden cocktails at Echo Lake is one such time.

More blasphemy: Ticket Central has those Bud Light margaritas I have grown to appreciate. There was a time when I would revoke my own annual pass for entertaining the idea of drinking pre-made margaritas from a can, produced by Budweiser. Compounding the crime, the incomparable Derby Margarita is sold right next door.

I credit the influence of a dear friend—we'll call her Sarah—with the fact that I would even consider something so unlikely. Her delightful family has one of those can't-miss houses on Halloween. They have the best candy, a fire pit, a welcome embrace and captain's chairs in the driveway for weary grownups, and a secret stash of 8 oz. Ritas for those in the know. Standing in the welcome shade of the Ticket Central awning, enjoying the 16 oz. strawberry version, I am struck by the unshakable irony of the situation.. On these days, and every Halloween, a Bud Light Rita falls just short of mollifying the guilt of knowing your family, who does not share your enthusiasm for convenient margaritas or captain's chairs, is getting farther away by the second.

Notable Potables

SweetWater 420 Extra Pale Ale
16 oz. can

Bud Light Lime and Straw-Ber-Rita
16 oz. can

Tune-In Lounge
Echo Lake

Your family, which will just as soon leave you as wait for you to get a drink, is also probably going to ignore your advice about not spending hours to eat. When they commit you to the interminable wait for 50's Prime Time Café, deliver a hearty helping of I-tried-to-warn-you by ducking into the adjacent Tune-In Lounge.

50's Prime Time and Tune-In open at the same time, and Tune-In carries all the same delightful beverages. Indeed, the restaurant gets it drinks from the Tune-In bar. You can cut out the middleman by simply taking a seat in the lounge, though that denies you much of the charming service and 50's atmosphere. Yes, the lounge has wonderful service, as well as kitschy furniture, though the coverage isn't as complete, and the bartender has less time to dedicate to the whole theme and spectacle.

Notable Potables

Dad's Electric Lemonade
Skyy Vodka, blue curaçao, sweet and sour, Sprite, and a souvenir glow cube

Cigar City Brewing Jai Alai IPA
16 oz. draft

Goose Island 312 Urban Wheat Ale
12 oz. bottle

CHAPTER THREE

Disney's Animal Kingdom

I am convinced Disney keeps the Animal Kingdom 8-20 degrees warmer than the rest of the resort. With the exception of January showings of Rivers of Light, the park is too hot. However this is accomplished, it has resulted in a proliferation of frozen drink dispensaries. There are more places to get a drink here than in Epcot, and that is saying something.

Dawa Bar
Africa

A positively charming place to have a drink, if you sit in the right spot. Dawa is an open-air patio bar, which automatically garners my interest and affection. Dawa provides welcome relief for guests making the often unwelcome lengthy trek required to get between any two spots in this intriguingly designed park. It is also an oasis for anyone trying to get into Tusker House without a reservation. Certain seats become less pleasant at certain points during the day as the unforgiving sun makes its way around the grounds.

Before, during, and in the wake of decades tending bar, one drink upon which I pride myself is the Bloody Mary. There are infinite means of assembling a Bloody Mary. It would surprise the unfamiliar how many of them are not that good. With care and the proper ingredients, a Bloody Mary can be an exceptional drink. Olive juice is essential.

Dawa offers several Bloody Mary varieties. One of them carries the name of the lounge. The better one, Discovery

Island, contains olive juice. It's the one you should try. If you don't like Bloody Marys, you haven't had a good one.

Notable Potables

Discovery Island Bloody Mary
Snow Leopard Vodka, loaded Bloody Mary mix, lime juice, and olive juice, garnished with parsley and a skewer of mozzarella cheese, tomato, basil, and stuffed olive

Safari Amber Beer
16 oz. draft

Tusker Lager
16 oz. draft

Dino-Bite Snacks

DinoLand

I have been going about this all wrong. I have been smarmingly critical of Bud Light, when this is truly a moment to embrace the St. Louis spirit. Look at this from the perspective of people who like Bud Light. They couldn't be happier. It's available everywhere, and it's always the cheapest thing on the menu.

Surrounded by DinoLand mayhem is hardly the place for an elaborate cocktail. As part of a family you won't have time to enjoy it, and if you don't have kids, you ought not hang out over here anyway. Snatch up a beer, your little hooligans, if you have some, and retreat to more peaceful confines.

Notable Potables

Key West Sunset Ale
16 oz. draft

Drinkwallah

Asia

Areas within Disney World, the oft-enclosed, paved, and sheltered environs, can swelter even on a nice day. Certain Animal Kingdom pinch points appear to pay homage to the climates they represent, and can get positively hostile.

Crossing from Discovery Island into Asia, guests receive a welcome, if brief gust of relief from a breeze off the river. About a step and a half beyond the bridge, the wind disappears, along with all the oxygen. I've been hot here in January.

The excruciating climatic anomaly may have something to do with why Kali River Rapids is so popular. It just becomes that much more desirable when you are sweating blood.

The other line you encounter here is for the Yak & Yeti Restaurant. The wise made reservations and are inside out of the heat. The rest of us are attempting to crowd into Drinkwallah for slushie respite. Do not even read the menu. Pick anything. If you don't like what you get, pour it onto your shirt.

Notable Potables

Coconut-Lychee Lemonade
Parrot Bay Coconut Rum, Odwalla Lemonade, and lychee

Frozen Coca-Cola with Captain Morgan Spiced Rum

Flame Tree Barbecue
Discovery Island

Aptly named, this quick-service counter roosts beside one of several scalding Animal Kingdom thoroughfares. While the heat makes you want to simply lay down and get on with the business of catching fire, the smell of this glorious grill compels one to carry on, if for just one last meal.

Arguably the most underrated cocktail at the Disneyland Resort, Fillmore's Pomegranate Limeade from the Cozy Cone in Cars Land, is a simple, yet brilliant mix of juice and Skyy Vodka. At least it used to be. I can't get confirmation on the brand, now. Might be a licencing issue, though it still tastes like Skyy. Flame Tree Barbecue seems an equally obscure place to find a beverage so understated, yet divine.

Mandarin Orange Vodka Lemonade sounds simple. It's not. At any rate, I can't seem to replicate it at home, despite believing I have the exact recipe. It's just like the Dole Whip Float; another piece of the unattainable folklore that makes Disney so ineffable and wonderful.

Notable Potables

Mandarin Orange Vodka Lemonade
Skyy Mandarin Orange Vodka with ripe flavors of tangerine and lemon zest

Safari Amber Lager
16 oz. draft

Harambe Market
Africa

In my quest to get the kids to be a little more culinary adventurous, I almost had them convinced Animal Kingdom did not trade in pizza and hamburgers. Then, from halfway across the park, the boy spots someone coming out of Harambe Market with a corndog. Sigh.

At least Harambe Market also has Tikka Masala, ribs, and Reef Donkey APA. I couldn't get the kids to eat the former, couldn't convince my wife to get her own ribs, nor would the lot of them go to Rafiki's Planet Watch without me, leaving me free to enjoy my fill of the latter.

Notable Potables
Leopard's Eye
Snow Leopard Vodka blended with kiwi- and mango-flavored Bibo

Reef Donkey APA
16 oz. draft

Isle of Java
Discovery Island

While half the park's thirsty guests descend upon Drinkwallah, drawn by enticing, old-style Coca-Cola signage and the prospect of ice, the wary detour toward an unsung oasis behind Flame Tree Barbeque.

If you're not sure what to get, perhaps try a Coca-Cola Frozen Alcoholic Beverage. No kidding. That's what it's called on the menu. Not a typically Disney creative name for an item, right? Perhaps, given its offerings, or location, Isle of Java suffers from particular translation difficulties. At least with Coca-Cola Frozen Alcoholic Beverage you know exactly what you are getting.

Notable Potables
Island Cappuccino
Includes white chocolate and Captain Morgan's Spiced Rum

Coca-Cola Frozen Alcoholic Beverage
Includes Captain Morgan's Spiced Rum

Nomad Lounge
Discovery Island

There are certain signature attractions, views, and venues that define Walt Disney World: Spaceship Earth, California Grill, Cinderella Castle, Hoop-Dee-Doo Revue. Also, as in the case of Be Our Guest, we witness how Disney creativity shapes many restaurants into attractions themselves.

As much for the experience as the food, certain restaurants, pool bars, and taverns appear on your every-visit must-do list. For those who've discovered it, Tiffins has become one such place within Disney's Animal Kingdom. The attached Nomad Lounge is now a personal favorite.

I think I would have loved it, even if my first visit wasn't on a sweltering autumn afternoon. Nomad Lounge is the sort of place to which I travel when I am daydreaming. Rustic, dark-ish, littered with character and distraction. (I also dream about the contempo-modern, brightly lit California Grill Lounge, but, hey, diversity is a sign of sophistication, right?)

I love the theme, as well as walking in the footsteps of ambitious adventurers, and the very cast members who wandered the globe, turning another Disney dream into reality. My first crack at writing was composing family travel journals as a kid. I was disappointed when National Geographic failed to publish my eight-thousand-word Yosemite masterwork. Can't claim to be surprised, especially when my own family's interest was, at best, fleeting. I try not to hold a grudge. Not their fault they weren't blessed with a pioneer's vision and spirit.

I still adore the classic Disney specialty drinks menu. This has more to do with sentiment than any continued interest in the now arguably stale cocktails. The new Nomad Lounge menu is as brilliant as it is spiritually and physically refreshing. Even though it still hurts to think about Nat Geo and my pandering family, the menu's travel-journal format, reflecting emblematic Disney creativity, elicits predominantly positive sentiment. The beverages themselves will have you lining up outside Tiffins, waiting for rope drop.

Those of a mind, or adolescence, to order a non-alcoholic specialty beverage, I recommend the Zingiber Fizzie. Besides being a positive pleasure to say out loud, a Zingiber Fizzie is an exceptional drink. It is the unleaded version of the Annapruna Zing (also fun to say), described below, from the Indonesia pages of the journal. The Annapruna is ridiculously good. It is exactly what you envision when you taste the Fizzie and muse, "This would be something with some gin in it."

For atmosphere, aperitifs, and appetizers, you are unlikely to find anyplace as amazing as California Grill. Without meaning to, perhaps, in the Nomad Lounge we have stumbled upon one. I wish Nomad wasn't so far from the park entrance. I wish it wasn't so enticingly close to Pandora.

It is a must-do. I will come here every time I visit Walt Disney World. I will sip creative, whimsically colored cocktails, with intriguing backstories, as the less mindful pass by to fill prohibitive Pandora queues. I will fret, with pettiness unbecoming a Disney park, as Pandora flunkies spill over into my intimate, beautiful bar. I will take advantage of copious tipping, that the Nomad cast may remember me for all the right reasons, and I will get my drinks ahead of the masses.

Do not believe you can bribe a Disney cast member. But if it comes down to a coin flip between someone huffing and waving a menu like a fly swatter, or someone they recognize, who has been patient, and, in the past, memorably generous, who do you think gets their elaborate drink first?

Notable Potables

Annapurna Zing, Indonesia
Bombay Sapphire East Gin, passion fruit purée, mint, simple syrup, and lime Juice, topped with ginger beer

Jenn's Tattoo, Asia
Ketel One Vodka, watermelon, hibiscus, and lime juice

Kungaloosh Spiced Excursion Ale
USA, 16 oz. draft

Tiffins

Connected to Nomad Lounge, geographically, and via the combined intricate theme, Tiffins is more than a restaurant.

Some restaurant/lounge combinations get territorial. They share an entrance, some paneling, and a few beams, but then that's it. When the doors open, they are as individual as the accountants say they are. If you are sitting on the patio, don't expect bread or water from the crew inside, and vice versa. That's rarely the case at Disney, and certainly not here. Tiffins Restaurant and Nomad Lounge co-exist in a manner that completely considers and benefits their guests.

Most important, they share the extraordinary specialty cocktails menu. It's a slightly different experience, but Dalang's Delight on Nomad's patio tastes equally wonderful at a table inside Tiffins exceptionally appointed dining room.

Notable Potables
Dalang's Delight
Starr African Rum, Batavia-Arrack Van Oosten, Van der Hum Tangerine Liqueur, Mountain Berry Tea, simple syrup, and lemon juice

Alta Limay Select Pinot Noir
Argentina (glass/bottle)

Pandora—The World of Avatar
By not seeing Pandora, I'm a little confused by all the bizarrely colored food, drinks, plants, and creatures purported to be everywhere. Despite my unshakable love for Disney, I don't think it's necessary to sit through another two-hour James Cameron movie just to understand why Animal Kingdom now serves bioluminescent green beer.

Pongu Pongu
For the novelty alone, even the Pandora quick-service counter is worth a visit. As the new attraction wait times continue to frustrate, an exotic Pongu Pongu libation will help settle and salvage your mood. If it keeps you out of my favorite cozy chair at Nomad Lounge, I will send people here all day.

The beverage menu is as inspired as the decor, and the all-encompassing new land. When the initial crowds taper off, we may not even mind how much of a round-about route it takes to get over here. Until then, find solace in the wonderful beer and odd cocktails.

Notable Potables

Hawkes' Grog Ale
Golden ale with brilliant green color and flavors of wheat and citrus followed by a creamy finish, in a 22 oz. draft and for three bucks more it comes with a Glowing Unadelta Seed

Mo'ara Margarita
Sauza Commemorativo Añejo Tequila with strawberry and blood orange flavors topped with strawberry boba balls, again with the option for a Glowing Unadelta Seed

Satu'li Canteen

A 22 oz. Pandora draft beer costs only $1.25 more than a 16 oz. Pandora draft beer. Yes, Satu'li Canteen has a charming design, decor, and backstory, and when it's not too hot, it's one of the park's best patios. The availability of Disney draft beer for 20 cents/ounce, though, is most noteworthy. (It's not 20 cents for every ounce; just for the difference.) In light of almost every other Disney drink, which cost in the double digits, even an artificial discount represents an enviable deal.

Satu'li pours their Bloody Marys with Absolut Peppar Vodka. Just as with Van Gogh Vodka, available at Mama Melrose's Ristorante in Disney's Hollywood Studios, when you find an exceptional spirit, mixed within its ideal recipe, get it.

Notable Potables

Bloody Mary Cocktail
Abslout Peppar Vodka with spicy Bloody Mary mix and a micro carrot garnish

Banshee Chardonnay
Aromas and flavors of apple, pear, citrus and hints of vanilla

Banshee Pinot Noir
Ripe cherry, raspberry, and floral characteristics with a silky texture

Mo'ara High Country Ale
Amber ale brewed for the nature lover with herbal spice hop aroma and a malty flavor profile featuring notes of caramel, toffee, and nuts, in 16 and 22 oz. drafts

CHAPTER FOUR

Magic Kingdom

For decades, guests could not drink at the Magic Kingdom. As in Disneyland, the opinion was to keep the predominant family park free of alcohol, of drinking clubs, and the infamy each may inflict. Recently, slowly, the press of guest preference and profit margin have wrought unexpected changes.

With hard-earned reservations at a couple of fairly exclusive restaurants, guests are now granted temporary access to beer, wine, and some specialty cocktails. The same is true at Disneyland. In fact, it's ever harder to drink there. Make all the reservations you like at the fabled Club 33. You aren't getting in unless you know, or happen to be one of, the right people.

In either park, you are not permitted to walk about with a beer, or even a whimsical glass of blended bliss. The tippler in me laments the loss of a splendid adult opportunity. People watching from the elevated, outdoor Tomorrowland Terrace is a tradition and a delight. I can't help but think what a welcome glass of wine would lend to the experience, and to my hasty impressions of strangers who catch my discriminating eye.

The sentiment in me, the childlike enthusiasm stirred by anything Disney, is in favor of measures that limit the number of drunks inside the Magic Kingdom. There are plenty of places to be an adult at Walt Disney World. I would love a beer with my Columbia Harbour House Land and Sea Trio, and perhaps if I ever get stuck in the Space Mountain standby mayhem again. Truly, though, I am okay without the sight, smell, and sometimes unpleasant behavior that comes with freely available, if expensive, alcohol. We've all seen what the Drinking Around the World craze means for Epcot on a Saturday afternoon.

I'd just as soon nothing like that ever happens to the Magic Kingdom or my childhood memories.

Plan ahead and limit your drinking to a well-appointed (of course) table-service restaurant, and you shall enjoy a rare, enviable Magic Kingdom experience. Do pace yourself, and don't try to take a wine bottle over to the Tomorrowland Terrace. Disney cast members are accommodating, and sentimental themselves, but they aren't going to let you loose in the Magic Kingdom with booze on you.

Be Our Guest

The current menu is bristling with French and Belgian beer and wine. You are entirely welcome to enjoy a glass of Syrah from Walla Walla, Washington, if only for the specific joy of ordering it. I recommend you give into the setting and, yes, the palatial splendor. Have a true glass of champagne, or burgundy, from Beauty and the Beast's native land.

It's been around for ages, though Belgian beer is still an acquired taste, and is unfamiliar to many. Be careful not to derail your fairytale meal with an undrinkable mug of that beer your friends like, which you've never tried. Stella and Kronenbourg inhabit the lighter end of the spectrum, offering just enough European spirit to satisfy one's sense of adventure, without scorching the palate.

Notable Potables

Georges Duboeuf Beaujolais-Villages, Burgundy
Glass/bottle

Helfrich Pinot Gris, Alsace
Glass/bottle

Kronenbourg 1664, France
16 oz. draft

Stella Artois Cidre, Belgium
16 oz. draft

Cinderella's Royal Table

If you came here to drink, you need someone with professional experience to look after you and your money. It's a character meal, and I usually prescribe Bloody Marys for such encounters, but I doubt you can get one here. You can, however, get champagne as part of an enhancement.

The dining room is spectacular. If you get in, for your kids or an unparalleled view of the fireworks, order a bottle of bubbly. When making reservations, check the current and impending policy. By the time your visit comes around they might not be doing champagne any more, or, fingers crossed, they could have a full bar. Have other reasons to eat here, if you're considering it. This place has so much to offer, and is a little pricey for your decision to be based upon availability of booze.

Notable Potables

Rosa Regale "Sparkling Red" Brachetto d'Acqui
Piedmont (glass/bottle)

Jungle Navigation Co. Ltd. Skipper Canteen

A little lighter on the splendor, perhaps, but then, it's a little easier to get a table. The Canteen is every bit as committed to its theme, and you can put the food up against any restaurant this side of Cítricos. As your table comes with privileged access to wine and beer, the mere fact you are not surrounded by Cinderella Castle or the cast of Beauty and the Beast is easy to forgive.

The alcoholic options are serviceable. That is to say, since you get to have a drink at lunch inside the Magic Kingdom, they are wonderful. The major temptation, and thus drawback, is the enticing non-alcoholic beverage list. Pretty much everything on there would make an excellent cocktail. Unfortunately, no amount of pleading will convince any cast member in the place to bring you a Schweitzer Slush with vodka in it.

Notable Potables

Blue Moon
16 oz. can

Don Miguel Gascón Malbec
Mendoza (glass/bottle)

Liberty Tree Tavern

Nearly fulfilling my dream of having a beer with my Columbia Land and Sea Trio, Liberty Tree Tavern requires a bit of a commitment. It is thus better-suited than Columbia Harbour House to serve alcohol. Specifically, it is a little pricey, generally requires reservations, and you will eat too much to get drunk.

The decor would have thrilled a historian like Walt, and will keep guests coming back to experience the many monumental dining rooms. Children looking for beasts and princesses will cry in their cobbler, or throw it at you. The proud patriot, though, may bask in the glory of our founders, and a tall glass of fermented freedom.

Notable Potables

Iron Horse Fairy Tale Celebration Cuvée Brut
Green Valley, Sonoma (glass/bottle)

Sam Adams Boston Lager
16 oz. draft

Aloha Isle

As little as I truly want free-flowing alcohol inside the Magic Kingdom, what we have in Aloha Isle is a missed opportunity. A Dole Whip Float with rum is a delicacy well worth the miniscule potential risk involved in introducing it into your signature family fun park. The line will be so long, it will be difficult to get intoxicated off them, even if that was your dubious intention.

I put it to Disney that no one is foolish, or desperate enough, to get drunk exclusively from Dole Whip Rum Floats. Still, it is wise not to underestimate the foolish and desperate. Then again, if you were of a mind to get drunk in this fashion, are you going to be dissuaded from doing so by the simple absence of opportunity? Magic Kingdom security is surely alert for anyone spiking their smoothies behind Walt's Enchanted Tiki Room.

I believe I have a solution. They could serve the rum float in a special cup, for which you have to surrender your Annual Pass, MagicBand, or admission ticket. To get your pass back, or another drink, you have to face the scrutiny of specifically trained cast members. There will still be fools willing to give up their ticket at the end of a day, though the generally well-behaved public will take that opportunity to enjoy a delightful grownup beverage like responsible adults.

Disney, that idea is yours if you want it.

CHAPTER FIVE

Disney's Water Parks

If there is a Walt Disney World pursuit less suited to a family theme park than the excesses of Drinking Around the World, it's drinking to excess at a Disney water park. Fortunately, most of your more dedicated drinking clubs aren't willing to shell out the extra few dollars required for the water park hopper option. The twenty, or so, alcohol dispensaries, between the two water parks, present a serious temptation.

Considering what could easily be an excusable afterthought, Disney puts quite a bit of thought into their water park snacks and beverages. I saw gyros on a Blizzard Beach menu, and one of the piña coladas at Typhoon Lagoon has midori in it. Don't worry, Bud Light flows like chlorine through the kid's pool; pretty much exactly like it. The point is, there is a wider variety than you might expect. There are also hundred-foot drops, and some very real drowning potential. Pace yourself, like always, especially here.

Disney's Blizzard Beach Water Park

It's just a matter of time before this place goes fully Frozen-themed, right? A properly designed and delivered Frozen park, even merely a water park, will draw more guests than the increasingly maligned Hollywood Studios, Star Wars or no.

Wear sunscreen. You get twelve hours of sun in Florida, even on a rainy day. Wear sunglasses. The winter effects at this park are charming, though the glare they produce would blind a mole.

Arctic Expeditions

The initial case that makes our earlier point. Arctic Expeditions is a food truck—food snowplow, really—at a water park, and it offers better food than most table-service restaurants in my neighborhood. Either I need to move, or Disney continues to outdo itself throughout the resort.

Cheese steak, chicken gyros, craft beer, salads; I eat better here than I did all through college. Again, this does not reflect as well on my life choices as it does Disney's infallible attention to detail and guest comfort.

Notable Potables

Bell's Oberon Ale
16 oz. draft

Schöfferhofer Grapefruit
16 oz. can

Avalunch

Cleverness is a hallmark of Disney Imagineering and daily operations. From an entire water park based in the Arctic Circle to a gyro-dispensing snowmobile to each cleverly named attraction, snack shack, and entrée, creativity and deep thought accompany every Disney detail.

Avalunch may be a modest example, yet it works on so many levels. My thoughts, if anyone asks, here and at the other whimsically named snack stands, perhaps they could do with a couple more exotic beers.

Notable Potables

Yuengling
16 oz. draft

Beso Del Sol Sangria

Cooling Hut

The park is not huge. It takes little time to walk from one side to the other. Still, the pavement can be unforgiving to those who misplace their footwear, making even standing in place difficult. The solution is to have more variety at every food and drink outlet. Specifically, I want some of that wonderful craft beer you find at Polar Pub (see below) to be available elsewhere in the park, even just here at the Cooling Hut.

Polar Pub is stuck off to one side, and the rest of the park is a light-beer wasteland. This is not a crime. I am simply bitter because it took me three or more visits to wise up and pick a chaise over by Polar Pub in the first place. Equally upsetting, it was not until after that I realized you can climb into Cross Country Creek from pretty much anywhere and drift to the pub.

Something else I learned: don't buy hummus from Cooling Hut and try to float to the pub, no matter how much you love the pairing of hummus and IPA. If an attentive cast member doesn't manage to dissuade you, the chlorine and pool water will surely discourage you from trying it ever again.

Notable Potables
Miller Lite
16 oz. aluminum bottle
Angry Orchard Crisp Apple Hard Cider

Frostbite Freddy's Frozen Freshments
For a frozen-themed fun park, I would have thought pretty much every concession stand would dispense blended margaritas. Well, this one does. It's also got about a dozen options and reasons for forgoing that foolish diet you've been considering.

It might be human nature, be you at a beach, pool, or polar water park, to give consideration to your physique, health, and the general shadow you cast on the family next to you. Frostbite Freddy's and I are here to put such silliness and vanity to rest.

Would you eat barbecue brisket nachos at the beach or public swimming pool? I think the common, hasty answer to that has much to do with the scarcity of truly appetizing nachos in such places. Freddy's has nachos, soft-serve ice cream, and the Disney-famous jumbo turkey leg.

The beer selection isn't mind blowing. Take your turkey flesh down to Polar Pub and make a satisfying meal out of it. Also, despite overwhelming temptation, do not drag food into Cross Country Creek. There are several water features between

Freddy's and where you would get out for the pub. Each of them will ruin an otherwise wonderful nacho plate.

Notable Potables

Yuengling
16 oz. draft

Frozen Strawberry/Lime Margarita

Piña Colada

Lottawatta Lodge

Drinking red wine in the sun, for me, is a guaranteed headache. This has mostly to do with a personal compulsion. I shan't condemn what may be the world's most popular adult beverage for my failure to limit my intake.

Lottawatta Lodge, another splendidly named eatery, offers red and white wine. For those of a slightly less impulsive inclination, a sangria on the sun deck ought to be a slice of fermented heaven.

I like to get a Frozen Blue Raspberry Lemonade and walk down to Polar Pub and make a little cast member magic. Here I stress "walk." It's only about three hundred feet from one to the other. Plus, this drink is really blue. You won't get it into the creek. Blizzard Beach lifeguards can spot it from the parking lot.

Notable Potables

Yuengling
16 oz. draft

Beso Del Sol Sangria

Woodbridge Chardonnay/Cabernet Sauvignon

Mini Donuts

This bungalow does not serve alcohol. I include it for those who have never been in the presence of mini doughnuts while they are being made. Go stand by the counter, or sit on a nearby picnic table, and simply breathe the bountiful air. Now, see if you don't order a few dozen. Try the raspberry dip. The combination is ridiculous, especially with the Yuengling you brought over from Lottawatta Lodge.

Polar Pub

Now this is what we expected to find all over the park. True, we can't fault Disney for not sharing our vision and questionable priorities. It is thus not surprising there isn't a bar at the shuttle stop. But, is it too much to ask for a few more appropriately themed taverns?

As the only true bar on the premises, Polar Pub is not the singles scene one might expect, and fear. Not cluttered with churros, chicken fingers, and, well, children, service is efficient and easy to come by. There is a full bar from which to choose, though, as everywhere else on Disney property, I point guests toward the featured specialty drinks.

The official Walt Disney World website currently states the Strawberry Margarita at Blizzard Beach's Polar Pub is "blended with Salsa Tequila." I am familiar with, and love, Sauza Tequila. I regularly mix margaritas with the versatile and delicious Conmemorativo Añejo variety. If there truly is a Salsa Tequila, I am not aware of it, but am intrigued.

The Grapefruit Margarita, from Disney's renowned specialty cocktails menu, is available, as is that menu in its glorious entirety. Polar Pub cast members will surely appreciate your discriminating taste, and delight in making this drink with Sauza, instead of Patrón. I know Patrón remains the rage, but in a flavored margarita, it lacks the boldness necessary. I welcome dissenion, though must warn you I have considerable experience in this regard, plus the backing of La Cava del Tequila's infallible crew.

Honorable mention would go to the Angry Snowball, for clever naming, though given the ingredients, I cannot recommend it for anyone drinking out in the Florida sunshine.

Notable Potables

Angry Snowball
Angry Orchard Crisp Apple Cider with Fireball Cinnamon Whiskey

Grapefruit Margarita
Patrón SIlver Tequila, Cointreau, and ruby red grapefruit juice

Warming Hut

Never judge a Disney snack stand by its façade. Nestled indiscriminately in the corner of a water park, Warming Hut is an unexpected multi-cultural haven. Not convinced? The menu offers "Entrées," and here's one of them: Carne Mechata with Empanada, Shredded Beef in Tomato Sauce with Rice, Beans, Plantains and Tzatziki. I've eaten at table-service restaurants with less.

And, hey everyone, Warming Hut has Bud Light. For the amount of scalding patio you have to cross to get to it, it's pretty cheap. They also sell Corona. Since you're feeling all exotic with your empanadas anyway, get that instead.

Notable Potables

Corona
16 oz. draft

Disney's Typhoon Lagoon Water Park

A slice of paradise within a resort that seems to trade on it. With every wonderful thing there is to see, do, and experience at Disney World, I have difficulty making my way to the water parks. Typhoon Lagoon is the type of place where I could spend all day, were it not for Epcot, the Magic Kingdom, Echo Lake, a thousand bars, restaurants, patios, acres of enviable footpaths, several boats, trains, and monorails etc.

If you have the time, freedom, and proper passes, check out Typhoon Lagoon. When you burn your body beyond practicality, head back to the parks, which is where you want to be anyway.

Leaning Palms

Home of the Whistle Wetter, Leaning Palms is one of a couple resort-wide locations where the non-alcoholic beverage menu outshines the adult version. A Blueberry Frozen Lemonade is a fine start to what would be an exceptional cocktail at this tropical-themed water park. Tragically, Leaning Palms has no liquor.

They've got Bud Light, naturally. To be fair, a tropi-cal-themed water park is not a bad spot for domestic light beer. Ever sit in the sun in central Florida? The best way to do it is surrounded by a water park. Even then you will perspire vital organs through your pores before long. IPA, my prefered beer, and most cocktails are not suited to these conditions. Margaritas are the most blessed of all outdoor beverages, though a margarita the way I like it might well make one pass out in direct Floridian sunlight. Light beer, as it may actually preserve life, might be the way to go.

Notable Potables

Beso Del Sol Sangria Red

Let's Go Slurpin'

A bar next to the wave pool. The only way to top it is if Disney finally sees the brilliance of my proposal to puts bars along the path of its lazy rivers. It's unlikely.

Let's Go Slurpin', then, remains my go-to. I don't visit here often, though when I do, I post up as near the bar as I can. Typhoon Lagoon cast members are as wonderful and accommodating as every other. They do take a dim view of my attempts at stretching a towel between multiple Let's Go Slurpin' bar stools to create a hammock. So, I commonly opt for the nearest available chaise.

This particular bar features a Typhoon Tilly. Strangely, it is not available at Typhoon Tilly's eatery (see below). It shouldn't be available anywhere, as it is just the type of health hazard that could find you face down in Ketchakiddee Creek. It's got midori, crème de banana and blue curaçao in it. Your diges-tive system will be fighting such a noble battle just keeping it down, you likely won't realize the effect it's having on your brain. Next thing you know, you're an unwelcome corpse in the kiddie pool.

If the Typhoon Tilly seems familiar to you, you have either already had an unfortunate brush with drowning, or you are aware of Disney's Banana Cabana specialty drink. It has a couple of different ingredients, though its makeup doesn't render it any more drinkable, or less life threatening. By their scent, either might make a reasonable sun lotion, but I suspect its most effective purpose is as embalming fluid.

That said, the beverage I do recommend has about twice the alcohol, tastes a lot better, and poses far less digestive risk. Anyone advising you to drink Long Island iced teas out of doors in Florida is someone you ought not take too seriously.

The Typhoon Lagoon version of this homewrecker of a cocktail is the Big Island Iced Tea. They use a splendid Maui Vodka; Hendricks Gin, which is, of course wonderful; Sammy's Beach Bar Rum; and Cointreau in place of mere triple sec. While drinking anything on this level, be cautious, remaining especially wary of the water. You may want to take a nap on the nearest chaise, or at the bottom of the wave pool. Try to resist both. I find a waterfall to the head is a fine way to compliment this manner of refreshment. Also, make a contract with yourself which waterslides you are and are not comfortable pursuing. Vodka, gin, rum, and Cointreau will assure you Humunga Kowabunga is not nearly as intimidating as it sounds.

Notable Potables

Big Island Iced Tea
Pau Maui Handmade Vodka, Sammy's Beach Bar Rum, Hendrick's Gin, Cointreau, and sweet and sour, with a splash of Coca-Cola

Mango Margarita
Patrón Silver Tequila blended with mango purée (I almost never promote a cocktail that buries Patrón in vast mug of juice or mixers, but this one works)

Lowtide Lou's

Years back, Epcot began offering a Grey Goose Grand Marnier Orange Slush. Long before the inception of the Frozen 5K, wary guests would make the walk directly from the front entrance to France, just to get one. The drink has undergone some recasting, though the Grand Marnier version remains incredible.

Not a tragedy, but Lowtide Lou's got the wrong slush. They're calling it a Grey Goose Le Citrón Slush. It's a little different, even than the reconstituted Epcot version. It has orange juice. I wish it had Grand Marnier.

Lou's is not open year 'round. You want to be aware of that before you grab a spot on the south side of the surf pool. It's the only concession location over there. It's not an excessive walk to the next snack stand, unless you forget your flip flops on a typical summer afternoon.

Notable Potables

Grey Goose Le Citrón Slush
Grey Goose Citrón Vodka and orange juice with sweet and sour

Corona
16 oz. draft

Snack Shack

Not long on frills, hence the name. The Snack Shack's unsung contribution to humanity is something called the Sand Pail. It's a bucket of ice cream that you may eat in the manner you've always dreamed of eating ice cream: with a shovel.

Let's Go Slurpin', back along the beach, is a far more diverse location to get a drink. Also, Typhoon Tilly's, right next door, has a splendid beer selection. If you are interested in a frozen drink with your bucket of ice cream, you're in luck, if inviting the mother of all brain freezes.

Notable Potables

Piña Colada
Don Q Cristal Rum blended with piña colada mix

Strawberry Margarita
Sauza Gold Tequila, triple sec, strawberry purée, and sweet and sour

Typhoon Tilly's

You may not expect to find the best sandwich you've had in months in a distant corner of a Walt Disney World water park. Locate the Disney Springs Earl of Sandwich location, and you can have exceptional sandwiches for every meal. In Typhoon Tilly's, however, an unheralded Turkey Pesto is simply waiting for you to accidentally discover it.

Everyone in front of you will order a fish or shrimp basket. The aroma of frying oil is quite compelling. Resist, and follow a healthier route. Toast your temporary health consciousness with another pleasant surprise from Typhoon Tilly's craft beer selection. It's limited, and seasonal, though there always seem to be a couple true gems.

Currently, Sea Dog Sunfish and Reef Donkey APA top the list. With clever nautical naming, these two fine beers might still be flowing during your visit. My hope is to connect the cast members in Disney Purchasing with my beloved Ballast Point Brewing Company.

Notable Potables

Sea Dog Sunfish
16 oz. draft

Reef Donkey APA
16 oz. can

CHAPTER SIX

Disney's Resort Hotels

You could, conceivably, spend days at Walt Disney World touring the hotel properties alone. Don't do this. Your family will rightly resent you if your visit does not involve copious park time. The most comprehensive, fulfilling vacation strikes a balance between the parks, hotels, pools, theaters, trails, boats, shops, "street" performers, and sundry activities. But mostly the parks, of course.

Most of the resort's top ten restaurants are not inside any park. At least half of the top lounging and people-watching spots are spread about the various hotel grounds. Something else that is not readily evident: pretty much every Disney hotel has a gift shop that sells hard alcohol by the bottle. They're not giving it away, though it is cheaper than you might expect for such things from a Disney hotel gift shop.

Check out the glorious, creative properties. Have dinner at a true hidden gem of a restaurant. Grab an inspired cocktail, enjoy it within an elaborate swimming complex. If you aren't driving, get a bottle for your room. Then get back to the parks.

Disney's All-Star Movies Resort

Not the most elegant, the All-Star resorts are undeniably among the most popular. An opportunity to stay at a Disney-owned and operated property is coveted by those who have their priorities in order. A Disney resort doesn't have to have a day spa or dolphins on the roof to be wonderful. If the difference is between staying at an All-Star property, or a Holiday Inn across town, I will take the All-Star a thousand times out of ten. The art in the lobby, the buses pulling up regularly to take you to the parks, and the charm and character permeating the grounds separate every Disney hotel from every other lesser property.

Unless you're staying at one of the All-Star resorts, you may not happen by them at all. If you are staying here, despite a lack of steakhouses and butler service, you will be the envy of everyone in a rental car on the I-4.

Silver Screen Spirits Pool Bar

It may not be flashy, but did you come for a drink or a pedicure? This pool bar is a full bar, and by definition, is beside a delightful pool. I deliberately did not say relaxing. All-Star hotels are family friendly, and the lobby-proximate pool is the property's pulsating heart. If you want some quiet and a cocktail, you either need to come after the pool closes, or roam the property. The lobby, buildings, and grounds are quaint and more detailed than the limited credit they receive.

Here and throughout Walt Disney World, do not let an understated venue throw you. There are few drinks you can order that a cast member can't make. Okay, you have to go to the Norway Pavilion to get Aquavit, but we're talking about something you'd actually want. Nearly every full bar at Disney World can produce any drink off the Disney specialty drinks menu. This includes the All-Star bars. They all have at least a couple worthwhile beers. Should that not be the case when you visit, chalk it up to an ever-changing selection, if only to save my judgment from being called into question.

A featured frozen beverage at Silver Screen Spirits is the Moscato Colada. It contains Moscato grape-infused vodka, blue curaçao and piña colada mix. Grape vodka is not the offensive purple soda you can no longer stand, but which your children now love. Mix it with pineapple, coconut, and blue curaçao, and you get a taste sensation to rival the most disagreeable popsicle. It's the type of drink people send back. It's a blended concoction, which means it's not simple to make.

Notable Potables

Coco-Jito
RumHaven Coconut Rum, coconut water, and fresh lime juice, topped with soda water

Yuengling
16 oz. draft

Alto Limay Pinot Noir

World Premiere Food Court

Even less flashy than the pool bar, but for a quick beer, you can't do much better than a hotel food court or gift shop. The selection isn't stellar, though there are always a fair amount of registers open. Each guest is driven by their own sense of need, of course. Sometimes it's worth having instant access to a grab-and-go light beer, rather than stand in line behind an entire coed softball team ordering blended drinks, one at a time, from a single, overwhelmed bartender.

Notable Potables

Coors Light
16 oz. aluminum bottle

Modelo Especial
12 oz. bottle

Robert Mondavi, Woodbridge Chardonnay, Cabernet Sauvignon

Disney's All-Star Music Resort

The setup and menu for each All-Star resort are similar. The differentiation and character come through in the decor. Each has its own charm. Guests may choose between them based upon where their passions lie, though it often comes down to availability and cost.

I stayed at All-Star Music and loved it, though I wish I'd researched the layout a little better. I would have tried to secure a room closer to the lobby, and thus the restaurant and shuttle stop. Who am I kidding? I certainly would have done that, as that is also where to find the bar, biggest pool, and arcade.

Intermission Food Court

Pizza, pasta, burgers; all standard fare. I admit I did not eat here, though surely would have had I been traveling with my dear family, rather than researching a food-and-beverage guide.

I got a coconut water, and refilled my soda mug every time I passed anywhere near here. I went specifically for chocolate milk once. I had a craving, and they carry it. They also sell beer. I got some of that, too.

Notable Potables

Blue Moon
12 oz. bottle

Heineken
12 oz. bottle

Robert Mondavi, Woodbridge Chardonnay, Cabernet Sauvignon

Singing Spirits Pool Bar

Here I found an unexpected treasure. Singing Spirits is virtually on top of the Three Caballeros Pool. This particular pool appears to be the extracurricular activity center of the entire resort. There was always some manner of Disney trivia contest going on at/in the pool, which you could clearly hear from the bar, surrounding tables, and, to be honest, all the way back to my room. If there's one thing I enjoy more than Disney trivia, it's being on the periphery of a Disney trivia contest, at a pool bar, where I can participate on my own terms, with a drink and without having to interact with strangers or get called on.

Notable Potables

Apple Mule
Crown Royal Regal Apple, DeKuyper Pucker Sour Apple, and fresh lime juice, topped with ginger beer

Henry's Hard Orange Soda

Michelob Ultra
16 oz. aluminum bottle

Disney's All-Star Sports Resort

All-Star Sports was undergoing a remodel while I was there last. Unless they snuck in another ESPN bar or restaurant, I expect it will still resemble its All-Star cousins. That is to say, it shall be serviceable, eye catching, and economically feasible.

One advantage, if you happened upon a bus that was going to all three resorts, is that it seemed to stop at this one first.

At any rate, it happened to me a couple of times, toward the end of a day's operations, as parks were closing. This was not a scientific study, though it did benefit me. As it turned out, my room at the Music was closer to the Sports lobby than the shuttle stop of my own hotel.

End Zone Food Court

No surprises here: reasonable hot food, some sandwiches and grab-and-go options, and various desserts. Beer and wine, in sealed containers, which you may take back to your room, are the biggest draw for Disney drinkers. You don't save any money going this route, but you can drink it at your leisure.

Notable Potables

Bud Light Lime
12 oz. bottle

Michelob Ultra
16 oz. aluminum bottle

Grandstand Spirits

Within the Grandstand Spirits photo gallery online, there is a shot of a cluster of margaritas. This instantly intrigues me. They each have fresh lime, salted rims, and appear to be topped with some manner of liqueur. With these qualifications, I hardly even mind that they're presented in plastic cups. I prefer a chilled glass. Who wouldn't? One unfortunate reality of any mindfully run pool bar: you can't have glass. Break a glass by a pool and they have to drain the entire pool. Considering the size and attention span of the crowds frequenting every Disney pool, every Disney pool would likely be getting drained several times a day. A plastic cup is a small price to pay to not ruin the swimming plans of hundreds of famlies.

Notable Potables

Black Cherry Lemonade
Grey Goose Cherry Noir Vodka, Odwalla Lemonade, fresh lime juice, and grenadine, topped with Sprite

Disney's Animal Kingdom Lodge

Van der Hum Tangerine Liqueur. It comes from the Cape winelands of South Africa. Disney prides itself on customer service. Creativity is an exceedingly close second. Details, such as adding a South African liqueur to beverages exclusively at the Animal Kingdom Lodge and the Animal Kingdom theme park, is a signature Disney move. Upon tasting Van der Hum in a margarita, I am prepared to weather a modest break in the authenticity to have it more widely available. A fine compromise might be to concoct a Van der Hum-focused beverage for the Outpost at Epcot.

Boma—Flavors of Africa

A restaurant like Boma presents an issue for me, and, specifically, this guide. It's wonderful; should mention that straight out. It's a buffet; a major contributor to it being wonderful. Unlike many Disney buffets, Boma does not offer character dining. While I maintain character restaurants are paradoxically the least appropriate and most necessary venues to drink, a non-character buffet causes me considerable difficulty. The issue: I almost feel guilty drinking here, and it's compounded when the food is this good.

What we have is all-you-can-eat Flavors of Africa, without the child- and character-driven mayhem to justify open-source Bloody Marys. The food is exotic and divine. It's almost a shame to waste calories on beer or a cocktail. I know, I'm almost ashamed to say it.

Boma and most of the Animal Kingdom restaurants feature South African varietal wine. If you must sacrifice internal capacity, do it with something enticing that you likely can't get somewhere else.

Notable Potables

South African Red and White Wine
Glass/bottle

Casablanca Premium Lager
Morocco, 12 oz. bottle

Tusker House Lager
12 oz. bottle

Cape Town Lounge and Wine Bar

Those not properly dressed, or not willing to wait for Jiko (next door), will be drawn here. Those put off by the immaculate lounge and the words "Wine Bar" may miss an opportunity. It's beautiful, but don't be intimidated. As a former restaurant lounge bartender, can I also request you don't bring your extended family into the bar in anticipation of quicker service?

Of course, you may absolutely bring your kids. Any areas into which children are not permitted are marked. The point I am making is not about children. My message to families is this: just because there is not a wait for tables in the bar does not mean you should automatically expect faster service in the bar. Bars often have less coverage than restaurants. Yes, you can sit down quicker. But, that one kid working the whole room may not be able to get to you as quick as you are expecting.

Once you do attract a server, try to have your order ready. I recommend one or more of the featured African wines. Plus, Cape Town as well as Jiko provide another opportunity to sample a delicious Van der Hum Tangerine Liqueur cocktail.

Notable Potables

Mt. Kilimarita
Sauza Gold Tequila, Van der Hum Tangerine Liqueur, citrus, and cranberry juice

De Trafford
Stellenbosch, Chenin Blanc

The Ruins
Robertson, Syrah and Cabernet Sauvignon

Jiko—The Cooking Place

Exquisite dining, Animal Kingdom style. If the wild boar and $15 salad don't scare you off, you are in for a true adventure. With items like elk and beehive cheese on the menu, this type of restaurant overwhelms me. I need to get over my trepidation, as they also have Wagyu and on-site wood-fired naan, which I love.

This is not someplace you are going to gravitate toward for drinks. Once here, though, it would be foolish not to enjoy one. And I will not stop over-promoting Van der Hum Tangerine Liqueur. Order it everywhere they serve it.

Notable Potables

Harmattan Cooler
Van der Hum Tangerine Liqueur, cherry brandy, and Nobo Whole Fruit Tisane

Zebratini
Captain Morgan Spiced Rum, Godiva White Chocolate Liqueur, Frangelico, Amarula, and a shot of espresso in a chocolate aebra-striped martini flass

Maji Pool Bar

You had me at "pool bar." This particular bit of paradise is a trek for anyone not staying in the north wing Kidani Village rooms. Those staying elsewhere are likely to end up at the Uzima pool, and no one will fault you for that. Maji guests will enjoy a lower-key, less intense experience, unless you post up too close to the slide or kid zone.

Disney pool bars are pretty standard, which is to say they are categorically wonderful. Maji has a bit of a rustic feel, as though you truly are in some out-of-the-way retreat. This pool is specifically kid-friendly. I am sorry if the frequency of young people rises beyond your liking during your visit. That's what the frozen concoctions menu is for anyway, right?

Notable Potables

Coco-Jito
RumHaven Coconut Rum, coconut water, and fresh lime juice, topped with soda water

Moscato Colada
Skyy Infusions Moscato Grape Vodka and Bols Blue Curaçao blended with piña colada mix (don't drink more than one of these without consulting a gastroenterologist)

Safari Amber Lager
16 oz. draft

The Mara

Grieving parents, losing the battle to broaden their children's culinary horizons, here is your salvation. For those families staying at Disney's Animal Kingdom Lodge, when your kids rebel against the sophisticated cuisine, when they simply won't take one more meal of unrecognizable chickpea-scented fricassee, release them to Mara's much more familiar fare.

Beware: Mara does have pap, chakalaka, potjie, and egg custard, and several of the chicken dishes carry exotic-sounding names. Your children will suspect you are up to something. Simply point the least credulous toward the flatbread station, and hope they become more adventurous back inside the parks.

Notable Potables

Safari Amber Lager
12 oz. can

Michelob Ultra
16 oz. aluminum bottle

Sanaa Lounge

There is a Sanaa restaurant, and it is outstanding. The Sanaa Lounge serves everything the restaurant does, and falls much more thoroughly within my comfort zone. It thus garners more of my consideration, custom, and the bulk of this review.

Indian-Style Bread Service is a confluence of terms that warms my heart much in the manner of "all-you-can-eat tacos" and "rooftop pool bar." Sanaa, both restaurant and lounge, offer a pricey, yet novel bread spread. Tiffins, and thus Nomad Lounge, have something similar, and increase my adoration of both. The Sanaa offering is better. There are more options, and several of the choices involve naan.

I don't want to promote straight loitering, but with food on my table, I always feel more comfortable lounging at length. A charcuterie or bread-service appetizer frees you to hang out. Order a drink, too. Then start making plans to come back here.

If you need any more reason to love Sanaa, it shares Nomad Lounge's extraordinary specialty drinks menu. I am always tempted to recommend wine with bread service, though wouldn't fault anyone for favoring something a little more creative, colorful, and complicated.

Notable Potables

Annapurna Zing
Bombay Sapphire East Gin, passion fruit purée, mint, simple syrup, and lime juice, topped with ginger beer

Malawi Mango Margarita
Zignum Reposado Mezcal, Van der Hum Tangerine Liqueur, mango purée, and fresh lime juice

Painted Lemur
Amarula Fruit Cream Liqueur and Van der Hum Tangerine Liqueur combined in a chocolate-striped glass inspired by the distinctive striped tail of the Madagascar lemur

Spice Route Chakalaka Red Blend
Swartland

Uzima Springs Pool Bar

There are certain locations within a Disney resort where you are almost prepared to violate long-standing Disney rules and trespass. Do not ever do this, first of all. But, as you're floating along on Frozen or Pirates of the Caribbean, or in a log jam on Splash Mountain, don't you feel an almost hypnotic compulsion to become part of the attraction?

The reason I even mention it is the desperation I feel to jump into the Animal Kingdom Lodge pool, despite not being a guest there. I understand the policy, and begrudgingly appreciate it. If I ever foot the bill for such a place, I am going to want the pool as exclusively to myself as it can get. Standing at the Uzima Springs bar, it's perhaps only the thought of chlorine in my $11 drink that keeps me out of the pool. Someday, though...

Notable Potables

Big Island Iced Tea
Pau Maui Handmade Vodka, Sammy's Beach Bar Rum, Hendrick's Gin, Cointreau, and sweet and sour, with a splash of Coke

Kona Longboard Island Lager
16 oz. draft

Victoria Falls Lounge

I could not wait to review this lounge. I almost led off the book with it. Guests are spoiled by Disney's consistently remarkable and creatively appointed dining areas. Disney restaurants, lounges, even elevators are attractions all their own. Victoria Falls is a whole other level of extraordinary. The place is so nice, I was afraid to sit down or touch anything.

I knew it was lovely, but what had me stampeding over here is Van der Hum Tangerine Liqueur. I have since learned, to my immense pleasure, that Van der Hum is available at Tiffins, and all over the Animal Kingdom property, though I first heard about it in connection with Victoria Falls Lounge, and specifically Mt. Kilimarita, "the ultimate African Margarita."

Judging from the ingredients, it looks like a recipe you might get off a box of wine. It's so simple, and contains Cuervo, the tequila equivalent of corn flakes. There is nothing wrong with Jose Cuervo, despite what those Ray Liotta ads are doing to the brand. Without exaggeration, or concern for what it does to my own reputation, I would choose Cuervo over Patrón, for a mixed drink, every time. I tend to go a different direction, though Cuervo holds up better than a lot of premium tequilas, which disappear if you put anything bolder than lime juice in them.

I was told, by the friend who first suggested Mt. Kilimarita, to order and drink it as-is. He said this particular tangerine liqueur makes enough of a difference, and not to mess with it. He was right. It's outstanding. Of course, I instantly began to consider how Van der Hum would compliment a better recipe. Fortunately, I was able to find one at Tiffins, inside Disney's Animal Kingdom. Yes, I went on at length about it (Dalang's Delight, above). I am not surprised my new favorite drink comes from the Nomad Lounge and has Van der Hum in it.

Notable Potables

Dalang's Delight
Starr African Rum, Batavia-Arrack Van Oosten, Van der Hum Tangerine Liqueur, Mountain Berry Tea, simple syrup, and lemon juice

Mt. Kilimarita
Jose Cuervo Gold Tequila, Van der Hum Tangerine Liqueur, and sweet and sour, with a splash of cranberry juice

Snow Leopard Salvation
Snow Leopard Vodka, pear liqueur, mint, and lime juice, topped with ginger beer

Xingu Black Lager
16 oz. draft

Disney's Art of Animation Resort

Every Disney resort has particular and distinct charm. You can count on creativity and maniacal attention to detail. You will stand in awe in the lobby, and in every room and restaurant within the Grand Floridian and Wilderness Lodge. You will also pay a premium to stay or even get a coffee at such properties.

Disney's Art of Animation, classified as a value resort, is a marvel and an absolute steal. As a result, it can be difficult to get a reservation for the length of any stay. The fortunate who secure rooms at this delightful property are the envy of fellow, less-organized bargain hunters. I am thankful to learn you can enjoy a Lynchburg Limeade by the Big Blue Pool, even if you aren't staying here. The lobby reminds me of the Rainbow Tunnel that used to be in the self-guided portion of the Imagination Pavilion before such things were removed.

The Drop Off Pool Bar

Nestled next to the fabled Big Blue Pool, the Drop Off is a tribute to the artistry of *Finding Nemo* and sun-dappled relaxation. An anonymous source informed me it's okay to hang out by most resort pools, you just shouldn't swim in them, or take up considerable real estate, unless you happen to be a guest.

Not that I would ever suggest crossing the fine line between stretching and outright breaking a Disney rule, but with flip flops and a whimsical cocktail from the Drop Off, you can pretty much pass for a guest.

A noteworthy display of whimsy: the Drop Off offers a beer flight. This is not an exceptional novelty, in a world replete with craft breweries and wine bars. This beer flight only contains one arguable craft beer and it's from Chicago. There's also a Budweiser product. I can't imagine purchasing it, except to pay off a bet. I list and comment upon it here for the pure hubris of featuring it on a Disney beverage menu.

Notable Potables

Blue Ocean
Bacardi Rum, Skyy Vodka, blue curaçao, Odwalla Lemonade

Beer Flight
Bud Light, Sam Adams Seasonal, Goose Island 312, Yuengling

Landscape of Flavors

Another of several food-court style eateries you will find around Walt Disney World, and not merely at the value resorts. The Contemporary and Coronado Springs each have one, as does Epcot, Saratoga Springs, the Dolphin, and others. They are quick, convenient, perfect for those on a dining plan, and they sell beer and wine. The selection is far greater, and better, at the pool bar adjacent to each, but there are times when a Corona or Coors Light will serve you just fine. This is where you find that, without the wait.

Notable Potables

Corona
12 oz. bottle

Michelob Ultra
16 oz. aluminum bottle

Disney's Beach Club Resort

At present, the Beach Club is undergoing a bit of remodeling. This happens, resort wide, from time to time. For this reason, I try to highlight not simply drinks I favor, but also those with a level of popularity that I feel will sustain them for years to come. Should any of them disappear on or before your own vacation, fault the overly ambitious Disney marketing minds, who never even consulted me.

Beach Club Marketplace

Currently a gift shop in the eye of the reconstruction storm. What's left of it has been forced into the corner of the lobby. It warrants mention in this guide, as I feel for the cast members piloting this floundering ship.

Forced right into clear view of everyone who walks into, through, and out of the hotel, the impromptu gift shop has become the de-facto information station. The happiest people in the hotel are those behind the front desk. For the duration of the remodel, they aren't the most visible cast members on hand. If you are just wondering if Beach Club Marketplace sells beer. The answer is yes; the selection just isn't stellar.

Notable Potables

Blue Moon
12 oz. bottle

Heineken
16 oz. can

Beaches & Cream Soda Shop

With an "Adult Hard Floats & Beverages" section on the menu, Beaches & Cream is truly for guests of all ages. Here's the trick: come here the first night of your visit, and your family will insist you come back every day. Now, here's the difficult bit: can you choose between dessert and a dessert drink? I have difficulty selecting a heaping chocolate lava flow over a creamy mint-stoked glass of wonder, and vice versa. My hope is always for someone in my party to order the one I don't, then kindly share.

The Grasshopper Float is a personal favorite. It's brilliant in its simplicity. I tended various bars for over a decade, and the combination of stout beer and mint ice cream never occurred to me. I don't feel wholly naïve, as it never occurred to anyone with whom I worked all that time, either.

Notable Potables

The Classic Root Beer Float
Coney Island Hard Root Beer with Vanilla Ice Cream

Grasshopper Float
Guinness Stout with mint chocolate-chip ice cream

S'mores
Chocolate and vanilla ice cream, Amarula Cream Liqueur, and Bols Creme de Dark Cacao, topped with marshmallow, chocolate sauce, and graham crackers

Cape May Café

Another festive buffet-style character dining venue. Guests are free to enjoy the experience with a beer, glass of wine, or something a little more influential off the Disney specialty drinks menu.

I always caution people in my party, or within my general well of gravity, to resist the Magical Star Cocktail. It's candy-like pink in hue, and has glow cubes in it. I am not specifically worried about kids trying to drink it, though this being a buffet, a cocktail can spend a fair amount of time on your table without direct adult supervision. My concern is for the poor cast member running the service bar. As soon as one luminous bright pink drink appears, everyone is going to want one. No amount of explaining how it is an adult drink is going to sway the dining room full of hooligans who now have a mind for it. Any drink mixer worth their name tag knows how to make a pink non-alcoholic beverage. That doesn't mean they should have to, nor should they be asked to waste an entire-shift's worth of glow cubes on one wave of pink, impulse-purchase Shirley Temples.

I also hesitate to recommend a Long Island Iced Tea at a Disney resort. With all there is to do and see, a sizable, four-alcohol cocktail can significantly alter one's itinerary, rarely for the better. If you are going to have one anywhere, it ought to be at a pool. I can make a special concession for the Beach Club Resort character restaurant. It's mere feet from arguably the best pool in the state. Even a hasty, compulsive consumption of a Cape May Long Island Iced Tea ought not to prevent you from finding your way out.

You aren't supposed to use the Yacht and Beach Club pool unless you are staying there. They check guests with irritating frequency. With a Long Island swimming through your brain, you will surely make a compelling case for why you ought to be allowed to stay, and how they can make themselves useful by bringing you another.

Notable Potables

Ultimate Long Island Iced Tea
Bacardi Superior Rum, Tito's Handmade Vodka, Hendrick's Gin, Cointreau, and sweet and sour, with a splash of Coca-Cola

Once Upon a Vine
California Red Blend

Hurricane Hanna's Waterside Bar and Grill

A mixed blessing if there ever was one. This bar stands as a welcome beacon for anyone passing between, or through,

Epcot and the BoardWalk. I tread these boards rather often. I favor Epcot's International Gate over the front entrance, and I do enjoy spending time around Crescent Lake, which is what Disney calls this particular bay.

Hurricane Hanna's is a convenient stop along the route, no matter your present direction. The drawback is that it sits right outside the sprawling Yacht and Beach Club swimming complex, and, again, unless you are staying at one of those resorts, you can't use the pool.

Most Disney hotels take a typically dim view of non-guests using the pool. Many swimmin' holes, like at the Polynesian or Bay Lake Tower, mock you from behind locked gates. As far as I have been able to uncover, Yacht and Beach Club is the only property that will bodily chase you from the area. They don't, actually. The cast member who came around and determined my MagicBand was invalid was extremely polite. She even rechecked it, as if we didn't both know I was trespassing.

You are quite free to stand on Hurricane Hanna's patio and long for splashing relief that is not forthcoming. The blessing and the curse: rather than walk out to the bar themselves, most of the lazy, fortunate jerks around the pool wait for servers. This makes them even more enviable and worthy of your scorn, but it also keeps the line short. A quick beer or blended drink helps renew enthusiasm for wherever else you were going.

Fair warning: dessing in your most obvious swimming attire and avoiding eye contact is not going to dissuade the kid with the whistle from checking your MagicBand. Trust me. Somehow they just know.

Notable Potables

Piña CoLAVA
Bacardi Raspberry Rum blended with piña colada mix and raspberry purée

Stella Artois
12 oz. bottle

Yuengling
16 oz. draft

Martha's Vineyard

With the surrounding, sprawling splendor, it can be difficult to find your way into this delightful lounge. I came in once, desperately fleeing the heat. I was rewarded with a wide-open table under a vent, and an unexpectedly bountiful salad. Then, to my infinite joy, there were several beers with which I was unfamiliar. I am always game to try something new. That's not true at all. I adore IPA, Bloody Marys, and margaritas. I haven't been comfortable straying from the tried-and-true since my brother-in-law introduced me to the wonderful world of sour beer. He's a brewer, and he knows his stuff. I am not entirely sure sour beer isn't an elaborate prank perpetrated by all our in-laws to get us to quit drinking.

Full credit for Boulevard for having one of the most enticing bottle and label combinations in the resort. Unaware of this particular brand, I decided to try it upon seeing the bottle behind the bar. It is undeniably not my brand of beer. Farmhouse ale is modeled after, or perhaps deeply ingrained in, the Belgian brewing style. It may well be an exemplary member of its class, it just isn't for me. Nice bottle, though.

Notable Potables

Black Pearl Oro Shiraz-Cabernet
Paarl

Boulevard Tank 7 Farmhouse Ale
12 oz. bottle

Disney's Boardwalk Inn

I don't know if I will ever make the financial decision to stay here, though I spend a great deal of every visit in and around the BoardWalk. As for accommodations and amenities, the Yacht and/or Beach Club would be my choice if I could ever make such a commitment to the area. Given the access to Epcot, and the many convenient and delicious food and beverage outlets, the BoardWalk itself is not to be overlooked, even if you aren't sleeping there.

AbracadaBar

Charm begins with the name on the sign, then beckons and follows guests inside. Those not keen on a themed lounge may be at the wrong resort. Those of a more appropriate and open mind, enjoy the campy confines, and equally clever cocktails.

With Big River Brewing right down the BoardWalk, it is interesting how AbracadaBar has such an inspired beer list, including one of Walt Disney World's best craft beers. Terrapin, an Athens, Georgia, brewery, has lent Recreation, their magical Session IPA, to the enchanting lounge. Lighter than a typical IPA, a session carries the full complement of taste. Try one. You'll crave it. You are going to be disappointed when you can't find it everywhere. It has yet to catch on in the manner of Goose Island, Yuengling, or Bud Light.

Notable Potables

Coney Negroni
Wild Turkey 101 Bourbon, Campari, and Carpano Antica Sweet Vermouth

Magic Hattan
Hudson Manhattan Rye Whiskey and Carpano Antica Sweet Vermouth

Orlando Brewing Blonde Ale
16 oz. draft

Terrapin Recreation Ale Session IPA
16 oz. draft

Ample Hills Creamery

Introducing alcohol into an ice cream shop ought to be disastrous. At a neighborhood mini-mall, in the hinterland of several schools, it would be. Within Disney World, and at the BoardWalk specifically, where most guests can walk, bus, or take a ferry back to their room, booze floats are a stroke of genius.

Beaches & Cream, on the other side of the bay, has a wider, and, I'll say it, better selection of adult indulgences. While waiting for your Trattoria or ESPN Club table, that may be a bit out of range. And, yes, I am absolutely advising you to get ice cream before dinner. It's okay. It doesn't count as dessert if it has alcohol in it.

Notable Potables

Hard Black Cherry Float
McKenzie's Black Cherry Hard Cider paired with a scoop of dark chocolate ice cream

Hard Root Beer Float
Coney Island Root Beer paired with a scoop of vanilla ice cream

Belle Vue Lounge

When you see the word "lounge" in conjunction with a Disney resort, you are in for something special. A southern California native, I have always been partial to the confluence of the words "beach," "pool," and/or "patio" with "bar."

While Disney beach/pool/patio bars are legendary, what they have done for the fine art of lounging at Walt Disney World forces me to re-prioritize my passions. Anyone skeptical as to how anyone else might rank a lounge over a patio bar needs to consider how unpleasant it can get outside in Florida. They should also pay a visit to Nomad Lounge.

Belle Vue is no Nomad, though is a little more convenient. Besides, with Pandora now open, the secret is going to be out on Nomad's Discovery Island hamlet. Semi-exclusivity was one of its advantages. No more. Belle Vue is close, comfortable, and does have a bunch of IPA on the menu. And, yeah, I will take a couch at Belle Vue over standing room and starvation anywhere else.

Notable Potables

Belle Vue Cosmopolitan
Belvedere Vodka, Grand Marnier, and cranberry Juice

Paul Hobbs Pinot Noir
Russian River Valley

Orlando Brewing I-4 IPA
Orlando, FL (16 oz. draft)

Sierra Nevada Torpedo Extra IPA
Chico, CA (12 oz. bottle)

Big River Grille & Brewing Works

A brewery at Walt Disney World is akin to cocktail service at a bowling alley. You may not have even considered how amazing it would be, and now that you've discovered it, your life won't be the same without it.

The food is wonderful (see Jalapeño Spinach Cheese Dip), especially for a grill, though that's only about the eighth best thing about this place. The beer, naturally, is a personal highlight. The selection is rotational, which is not uncommon for a brewery, and I advise returning guests to remain flexible. They can run out of a beer in the middle of your visit. It's no one's fault, except perhaps the fire marshall, who won't let them put fermenters on the roof.

Find two, or more, beers you like, just to be safe. There's also a full bar, and inspired wine list, though anything other than beer at a brewery is a little like cocktail service at the dentist.

Notable Potables

Gadzooks Pilsner
16 oz. draft

Steamboat Pale Ale
16 oz. draft

BoardWalk Joe's Marvelous Margaritas

Can you stroll past a margarita stand on the BoardWalk and not stop for one? I think I can, though don't feel it's worth the risk. Who knows when you might pass another. If you must know, the nearest outdoor margarita opportunity is from Hurricane Hanna's, at the Beach Club. Your Boardwalk Joe's margarita will be a pleasant memory by the time you get all the way over there. If not, you walk too fast.

Get the Grand Margarita. Yes, the other one comes with Patrón. Did you know, you don't really like Patrón? You think you do. Their PR people got to the right celebrities, and now you're content to drink less-fulfilling margaritas. Straight tequila drinkers probably prefer Patrón to Cuervo. They ought to. BoardWalk Joe's serves margaritas. Cuervo makes a better margarita. I will go to my grave saying that; hopefully with one in my hand.

Notable Potables

Captain's Seaside Sensation
Pineapple smoothie with Captain Morgan Spiced Rum

Grand Margarita
Jose Cuervo Tequila, Grand Marnier, lime juice, and sweet and sour, served on the rocks or frozen

ESPN Club

At a Disney resort, I rarely choose to patronize a chain restaurant. Nor would I go to Epcot and hang out in my own car. Okay, ESPN has way more to offer than the Epcot parking lot, I'm simply like the many who favor something new and unfamiliar over anything I can find at the Mall of America. Along those lines, if Disney puts in a Hooters, I won't go there either.

ESPN runs a wonderful sports bar. Those looking for pub food, good beer, and televised games will find it. All of those things can be found down the dock at Big River Grille. The food is better, so is the beer, and, depending upon the sporting event, it's often easier to get a spot in the bar. Technically, Big River is a chain. The only other locations are in Tennessee, if I'm not mistaken, which isn't convenient for me.

Notable Potables

The ESPY
Absolut Mandarin, peach schnapps, orange and pineapple juice, and Sprite

Dogfish Head 90-Minute IPA
Milton, Delaware

Funky Buddha Hop Gun IPA
Oakland Park, Florida

Flying Fish

This fine-dining restaurant, for which AbracadaBar is the lounge, may not necessarily draw you in for a cocktail. I completely understand if your Disney World itinerary does not include exquisite eateries. Even more, if you've only budgeted for and reserved one such meal, maybe make it in Epcot. Flying Fish is still worth a look-see. So, maybe come on in for a dessert, and of course, a drink.

You will likely have to wait for a table. The service and everything on the dessert menu will make it well worth your time. Plus, did I mention AbracadaBar and the BoardWalk are right there? You could do worse for places to hang out.

Notable Potables

Parlor Trick
Four Roses Small Batch Bourbon, simple syrup, and a splash of soda water, with fruit garnish

Veuve Clicquot Brut Yellow Label Champagne

Magic Hat #9 Ale
16 oz. draft

Jellyrolls

An actual Walt Disney World club. There aren't many places kids are not allowed, but this is one of them. It is essentially a dueling piano bar, and it's a blast. It is also seriously out of place. Day or night, I have never been at a loss for something to do at Walt Disney World, even when not using a park ticket.

Anyone of a mind to go, do it. You can't help but enjoy it. I am simply a committed lounger and wanderer, and can't see myself pulled into a club.

Notable Potables

Magical Star Cocktail
X-Fusion Organic Mango and Passion Fruit Liqueur, Parrot Bay Coconut Rum, pineapple juice, and a multi-colored glow cube

Leaping Horse Libations

A charmingly themed pool bar, you won't find it unless you're staying at the BoardWalk, or you decided to make the dubious walk between Epcot to Disney's Hollywood Studios.

In either direction, at a normal walking pace, the Friendship boats will beat you every time. I am wired like those who understand it takes longer to walk, but still can't come to terms with waiting for the boat. And I love those boats. Even on particularly humid days, a boat has to be in port, with no line on the dock, or I'm walking.

Leaping Horse is conveniently located right about the spot where the beverage I got from Hurricane Hanna's goes mysteriously empty. This is also the point where I tend to regret my decision to walk. If a Friendship boat would pick me up on this side of the Boardwalk Resort, I'd swim to it.

Notable Potables

Carousel
Absolut Mandarin Vodka and piña colada mix blended with orange purée

Beso Del Sol Sangria
Red or white; sold everywhere, though tastes particularly wonderful trekking that final furlong to Hollywood Studios

Michelob Ultra
16 oz. aluminum bottle

Pizza Window

Among my favorite phrases (see Lagoon Bar, free tacos, and all-you-can-eat lava cake), "pizza window" is right near the top. You may not get gourmet grub through a walk-up window, but it's quick, and it's pizza. The whole thing gets even better when it's at Disney World and it's also a beer window.

Those paying attention will surely guess the options are Bud Light, Yuengling, and seasonal Sam Adams. They've thrown in Moretti for a little authenticity. The only slight drawback is that the Pizza Window is right across from the specialty margarita kiosk. I love margaritas. Did I mention that? I love pizza. They don't go together anymore than tacos and Malbec. A reasonable beer is my choice here, over an exceptional margarita. That's hard to process.

Notable Potables

Moretti La Rossa
16 oz. draft

Yuengling
16 oz. draft

Trattoria al Forno

With a name like Trattoria al Forno, and resting as it does within the hinterland of Epcot's Tutto Italia and Via Napoli, one might hesitate to even approach another Italian restaurant. Do not be intimidated. Despite the authentic appointments and exquisite aroma, al Forno is eminently approachable. As the website says, it's "simply delizioso."

My research is as delightful as it is exhaustive, though it's possible I've missed an item or two. As far as I have been able to determine, Trattoria al Forno is the one place in the entire resort that carries San Diego's own Stone Ale. More specifically, they have Ruination IPA, a truly incredible product. They're asking a fairly dear price for a 330 mL. bottle of beer. Ruination is a double IPA, so at least you get considerable bang for those bucks.

Notable Potables

Sicilian Iced Tea
Amaro Averna Liqueur, Caravella Orangecello, iced tea, agave nectar, and fresh lemon juice

Sibona Chamomile Grappa
Fruity Italian brandy

Stone Ruination
330 mL. bottle

Disney's Contemporary Resort

Disney resort guests are the envy of everyone outside the sprawling splendor of Walt Disney World. The fabled hotels of the monorail loop, surrounding Seven Seas Lagoon, are at the peak of an even more enviable shortlist. The Contemporary, a timeless Disney World original, is more than just a fancy building with a monorail going through it. It contains what is now my favorite lounge, my favorite arcade, and is rather a fine place to get a drink and watch Magic Kingdom fireworks.

California Grill

Despite the menu, decor, and a spirit that endeavors to capture the essence of the Golden State, you will find that very little is actually from California. This is not an oversight or accident.

California has wonderful wine, produce, and cultural cuisine. I maintain that the very best beer is from California. It is also known for gathering the best from all other parts of the world and presenting it in a unique manner. From pretty much anywhere that is worth living in California, you can walk to an excellent Mexican, Japanese, Italian, Greek, Cajun, and seafood restaurant, deli, BBQ, and brewery.

Octopus sashimi, cauliflower silk curry, New Zealand venison, artisan tacos: California Grill emulates dynamic native diversity. It doesn't have to be from California to taste like California. The breath-taking view is also a tribute to the glorious Golden State, and the service is perfectly professional.

A California carpetbagger case in point: Santa Monica Cider. The primary ingredients are from Sweden and Scotland, but the taste and essence are pure southern California. Try one, pair it with Sonoma Goat Cheese Ravioli, or a nice Ostrich Filet (totally Cali), and enjoy the transformation.

Notable Potables

Rosemary Lemontini
Belvedere Vodka, lemon juice, rosemary syrup, Fever-Tree Bitter Lemon

Santa Monica Cider
Rekorderlig Strawberry-Lime Cider, Hendrick's Gin, agave nectar, lime juice, and micro basil

Amstel Light
12 oz. bottle

California Grill Lounge

The finest restaurants at Walt Disney World—Le Cellier Steakhouse, Cinderella's Royal Table, The BOATHOUSE, etc.—all serve Bud Light. Most counters and kiosks have it. Now, fresh off my my recent visit, I understand the best bars do, too.

I have, on previous occasions, been slightly discourteous regarding Bud Light. If you like Bud Light, Busch bless you, there is nothing wrong with it. But Light was served at my wedding. No, I didn't have one, but I knew there would be people there who'd insist upon it. For the record, they are all on my wife's side of the family.

My issue, if you can even call it that, is I have trouble imagining being somewhere like the California Grill, at the top of, and near the spiritual center and beating heart of, Walt Disney World, and desire a demure beer that you can purchase pretty much anywhere else in the world.

During an Ohio State tailgate party, at your uncle's for Thanksgiving, even at Mardi Gras, if that's your choice, drink light beer, absolutely. When faced with a rare opportunity to spend a few moments relaxing at an inherently unique venue, I encourage everyone to pursue food, beverages, even souvenir items that are going to lend to the rarity of the occasion and punctuate the special memory.

Just because California Grill offers beverages you've never heard of before, doesn't mean you have to order them. You can, if that's something you want to do. I've found it leads, fairly often, to unpleasant surprises. Read the specialty cocktail ingredients. If something piques your tastebuds and interest, jump on it. If not, trust the knowledgeable cast members to steer you toward a memorable glass of wine.

Notable Potables

Anaheim Mule
Hangar 1 Mandarin Blossom Vodka and Fever Tree Premium Ginger Beer with a splash of orange jice

Napa Blue Martini
Charbay Vodka and olive juice with blue cheese-stuffed olives

Coronado Orange Avenue Wit
12 oz. bottle

Chef Mickey's

Sequestered between a bar and the monorail station, behind the Contemporary food court, the placement of this particular character breakfast is befuddling. It's exceedingly popular. That's not the issue. I suspect I only bring it up as every time I come up to the Outer Rim, or, let's face it, the arcade, the entire floor is beset by strollers.

Truly, the placement beneath the monorail platform is well conceived. As a parent, as long as you are facing the correct direction, when you throw back your head in exasperation, it gives you something else to look at.

Every Disney character meal, from Disneyland to Paris to Bay Lake, offers a full bar, including the fabled Disney specialty cocktails menu. All you really need in these overwhelming venues is a Bloody Mary. They go perfectly with costumed chaos.

Peruse the menu, though. Something else might catch your fancy, and you can order that when your Bloody Mary is gone.

Notable Potables

Get a Bloody Mary

Cove Bar

An elusive slice of paradise. Also an enviable place to get a cocktail, for those with the proper MagicBand. Cove Bar is at the Contemporary's newish Bay Lake Tower pool, and is only available to guests of that hotel, plus Disney Vacation Club members.

Notable Potables

Black Cherry Lemonade
Grey Goose Noir Vodka, Odwalla Lemonade, fresh lime juice, and grenadine topped with Sprite

Modelo Especial
12 oz. pour

Outer Rim

Admittedly, not the most outwardly enticing lounge. This is primarily the fault of Chef Mickey guests loitering and using the area to bivouac their strollers. You have to sit in the bar, or neighboring lounge chairs (if you can get one) to appreciate Outer Rim. The Contemporary generally, and fourth floor in particular, is a splendid place to spend some non-park time.

You won't believe this, but they have Bud Light, Yuengling, and seasonal Sam Adams on draft. Perhaps in homage to the Polynesian across the way, they also have Kona Longboard Island Lager. Between that, Lagunitas IPA, and the full bar, Outer Rim is a splendid venue for a drink.

The view is terrific in many directions. From here guests may gaze out the window across Bay Lake, at Walt Disney World's glorious eastern expanse. Turn inward and marvel at the Contemporary's enormous, intricate murals you've heard so much about. You can use this vantage point for monoral spotting, if you are into such things.

Industrious guests awaiting a monorail to the Magic Kingdom, and points beyond, may enjoy a beverage at the Outer Rim, rather than up on the platform, where they prefer you weren't drinking. If there is a considerable wait for the monorail, there's not much you can do, aside from enjoying yourself in this delightful, wide-open lounge. With light crowds and a timer, you needn't wait at all, and you needn't be not drinking the entire time.

I haven't asked, and am not sure what the Contemporary cast thinks of guests drinking in the Game Station Arcade, the home of my favorite game, Galaxian. It is the only video game I am still good at, and to which I even know the rules. On the machine there's a sticker that says "SUITABLE FOR ALL AGES." Pretty sure that is not in reference to language or violence. Rather, I think it means old people can still understand and play it.

Game Station has Galaxian. I got the high score, eighteen years ago, when the Contemporary's arcade was in the basement. I think it still stands. There's something paradoxical about playing one of your favorite arcade games at Disney World, where you used to play it as a child, but now with an IPA balanced on the machine. With IPA in my brain, I'm not quite as good as I once was, though I am better than I have a right to be.

Notable Potables

Raspberry-Ginger Mojito
Finlandia Raspberry Vodka, ginger, mint, raspberry purée, and fresh lime juice topped with coconut water

Maschio Prosecco, Vento
Sparkling wine; makes an excellent mimosa, in case you're here waiting for a table at Chef Mickey's

Lagunitas IPA
12 oz. bottle

The Sand Bar

The Sand Bar stands at the intersection of two of my most ardent, conflicting passions. It's a pool bar that serves nachos. I don't believe one can have too much of a good thing, though clearly good things can exist in conflict. Like taking popcorn on Splash Mountain, something Disney fortunately will not let you do, some elements just don't mix, no matter how much you love them individually.

My problem is an inability to avoid those awful ball-park-style nachos. I say this as someone with unlimited access to incredible Mexican food. I know bastardized nachos are terrible for me. Anything that particular shade of cheese-sauce orange should not be ingested. Throw it on top of fried tortilla chips, with sour cream, perhaps, and it's a meal quite specifically not suited for a poolside patio. The pool-going public does not want to see other members of the general public eating cheese, ice cream, or hot dogs, in the sun with their shirts off. Unfortunately, Sand Bar serves all three, and I am addicted to each. Throw in several varieties of beer, and you have a significant outlet for my unavoidable, unwise compulsions.

As a courtesy to people who pay to stay at the Contemporary, I have made a personal pledge to no longer eat by that pool. I now take my nachos, as a distraction against the heat, as I make the walk between the Contemporary and Magic Kingdom.

Notable Potables

Grand Margarita
Jose Cuervo Gold Tequila, Grand Marnier, fresh lime juice, and sweet and sour

Sierra Nevada Torpedo IPA
16 oz. can

The Wave Bar

If this bar was closer to the arcade, it might be my favorite resort hang-out. Just typing that, I think I understand why it's not. The Wave is a popular place. If it and the arcade were on the same floor, it would irreconcilably change the whole dynamic. We'd run the poor kids out of there. They would be relegated to the smoking section behind the Convention Center. We can't so blithely gamble with the future.

Wave's lighting and decor, especially in the lounge alcoves, are inherently soothing. I can sit here and simply stare at the blue neon (probably shouldn't do that), and forget where I am or why I came. Try to recover your senses by the time a server makes their way to you.

The Wave has a full bar, and carries the delightful Disney specialty drinks menu. When I don't immediately identify a signature cocktail, I tend to gravitate toward local or a favorite craft brew. The Wave has lots of each. Orlando Brewing is a regular feature; at least it was during my last couple visits. Tampa's Cigar City is another semi-local fixture.

A cocktail on the menu that struck me, which I might have ordered had I not been suffering a neon-induced trance, is the Sake Martini. Not sure how I would like it, or how my body would react. It's not something I am used to seeing, which is why I would try it in a bar I visit so infrequently. We are often warned against mixing sake with anything else. Limit yourself to three or four of these, and you'll be fine.

For guests at the bar, note the size of the monolithic structure. Even for multiple bartenders, there is a lot of ground to cover. I got lost in the crowd here one night, and it wasn't that crowded. I don't blame anyone, other than my own countenance, which clearly failed to draw attention. I have long preferred to sit back at a table. I wonder if this is why. Comedian Demetri Martin claims his superpower is that he's invisible to bartenders. Wish I had thought of that first.

Notable Potables

Sake Martini
Karen "Coy" Sake, Licor 43, and Cruzan Mango Rum, with a splash of orange and pineapple juices

Cigar City Jai Alai IPA
16 oz. draft

Disney's Coronado Springs Resort

This resort is so far off the beaten path that most guests who aren't staying there never see it. This is also true of Disney's Caribbean Beach and the Four Seasons. And this is a shame. One hotel property is not nearly as compelling as any theme park. Still, if you have or can find room within your itinerary, time spent touring unfamiliar resorts is inherently well spent. A walk through Coronado Springs, savoring a frozen beverage, ought to be high on your list.

Café Rix

My temptation to breeze right to Coronado's outdoor bars fits my profile, though it does the lobby venues a disservice. Without remorse, unless you're headed up to your room, or want to grab a quick smoothie on the way to the shuttle, you can probably skip Café Rix. They sell beer and wine from a cooler, similar to your finer Disney food courts. If you just want a drink to tide you over on your walk around the property, step outside to Laguna Bar. Or, go to the Pepper Market food court itself, where you can get a sangria or draft beer.

Notable Potables

Corona
12 oz. bottle

Bud Light Lime
16 oz. aluminum bottle

Laguna Bar

When you add the word "bar" to any paradise-associated location, e.g., beach, pool, patio, lakeside, riverfront, or roof top, those places become even more wonderful. It helps complete the picture if there is also actually a bar there.

Appreciating my limited Spanish, I understand Laguna Bar to mean Coronado Springs has a lagoon with a bar next to it. Walking through the lobby, a lagoon becomes obvious. It is beautiful, and there indeed is a bar there; a lagoon bar. Forty-some years into my life, and this is my first lagoon bar. I clearly don't get out enough.

Were it not for the fact you can't swim in the lagoon, and Coronado already having a spectacular pool bar, one might well spend the day at Laguna. There is seating. There is also a variety of delightful eating options nearby.

For me, paradise becomes heaven with the simple act of putting my feet in the water. I am not advising guests to break Disney rules and wade into the lagoon. It is a bit of a trek from the lobby to the pool, however. Laguna Bar, then, is perfect for stocking up (getting a drink) for the walk ahead. It's a full bar. They have beer and wine, naturally. A walk through the customary central Floridian climate calls for a frosty cocktail.

This tiny bar by the bay has several creative choices. I opted for a Coronado Crush. It sounded delicious, and looked like something I might not find, in this exact combination, anywhere else.

Turns out it is delicious. So much so, I was delighted to find it offered at Siestas pool bar when I arrived, where I got another one. It's not a mixture I pursue, normally. The kind cast members will entertain substitutions, if you have them.

Notable Potables

Coronado Crush
Tequila, Chambord, raspberries, mint, club soda , and lime

Laguna Azul
Raspberry Vodka, blue curacao, sweet and sour, simple syrup, and Sprite

Yuengling
16 oz. draft

Las Ventanas

There might not be a more understated restaurant at all of Walt Disney World. Hidden behind Rix Lounge and the food court, ignored mostly because of Maya Grill and the pull from the bars outside, Las Ventanas may well be shuttered.

When I stay here, I am going to have Las Ventanas breakfast everyday. And not just in the morning. I am going to order Huevos Divorciados, Sourdough French Toast, and Chorizo Skillets as often, and as late into the day, as they will allow it.

It's not on the menu, and I am appalled at who I've become, but nothing pairs with Chorizo Skillet quite like a Michelada. You may meet slight resistance if your cast member server has never worked in a bar. Patiently describe how it's made, with lime juice, salt, pepper, and assorted hot sauces. They have all of it. If they can find Tajín, so much the better.

Notable Potables

Corona
12 oz. bottle

Modelo Especial
A prime Michelada component (12 oz. bottle)

Maya Grill

A native southern Californian, I am positively addicted to Mexican food. My conditioned predilection is for reasonably priced fare, served through a window, that I may order and enjoy in my bare feet, at midnight. I am not averse to gourmet alternatives, though am most often content to enjoy a taco on a bench somewhere.

Maya Grill is extremely nice. The menu is wonderful. If you are not surrounded by Mexican food outlets at home, consider treating yourself to a meal here. I am more apt to recommend any of the number of fine options within Epcot's Mexico Pavilion, because, well, Epcot. Until then, spend your calories and time at Siestas Cantina and the Pyramid pool.

Notable Potables

Pineapple Margarita
Tequila, ginger liqueur, caramelized pineapple nectar, fresh lime juice, and agave nectar, served on the rocks with a hibiscus Himalayan salt rim

Viña Maipo Cabernet Sauvignon
Chile

Dos Equis Mexican Lager
16 oz. draft

Pepper Market

Most resort food courts serve beer and wine, from a cooler. Not this one. Even Coronado's lowest-frills eatery stands apart by providing a bar. Technically, the bar is a coffee counter, but they serve beer and wine by the glass, and a delicious trio of blended margaritas.

Coronado Springs' cast members are as attentive and kindly as any other, though this coffee counter is kind of an afterthought. It's a little off to the side. Certain times of day, the café is not the highest priority. I hate to go ask for assistance. It's just a thing I have. My wife would like me to work on it. If you don't want to stand over here at the fake bar, thirsty and lonely, politely alert someone to your presence.

There is not a cast member on the resort who is going to ignore you intentionally. The apologetic kid who finally came to my rescue said he thought I was just reading the menu. "I was," I assured him, "and now I would like to order something from it." Without the slightest bit of attitude, he informed me I could approach a cast member from any other station, including the cash registers, and wouldn't have to wait next time. My wife has a point. Of course she does.

Notable Potables

Fiesta Margarita
Layers of lime, mango, and strawberry

Vina Maipo Chardonnay/Merlot/Cabernet

Orlando Brewing I-4 IPA
12 oz. bottle

Yuengling
12 oz. bottle

Rix Lounge

Rix is the reason you may have never been to Las Ventanas. Despite some wonderful dishes at the latter, we cannot blame you for gravitating toward this amazing, hypnotic cantina. For starters, it's beautiful. While I wouldn't list that as a requirement in choosing a bar, since Rix doesn't have a view, aesthetics is an undeniable asset here.

Comfort is also a prominent attribute. I do rank that highly. I don't care what's on the cocktail menu, and almost don't care about the prices; if your furniture elicits unpleasant middle-school memories, and posture, I'll go next door.

Rix has an extraordinary beer, wine, and specialty drinks list. It's also not expensive, at least not by Disney lounge standards. The only negative: you aren't supposed to take Rix glassware over to the Lost City pool. It's pretty much a crime to put a Rix cocktail in plastic, even for this really good cause.

Blessedly, you can get wonderful margaritas all over the resort. Experience one here and at the pool. Rix is an extraordinary martini bar, too, if that's your thing.

Notable Potables

Mango Blueberry Basil Margarita
Coconut rum, Tequila, orange juice, mango purée, blueberries, and basil, served on the rocks with hibiscus Himalayan salt rim

Margarita Flight
Five shot glasses of specialty hand-crafted margaritas: Mango
Blueberry Basil, Classic, Blood Orange, Pineapple, and Jalapeño

Rix Blossom Sparkling Martini
St. Germain Elderflower and grapefruit juice, topped with
champagne

Siestas Cantina

Siestas is Coronado's main pool bar. Each Disney World hotel
has its own pool. Many have several. Resort pools, and most
amenities, are intended for the exclusive use of guests of each
particular resort, but everyone, hotel guest or carpetbagger, is
invited to enjoy the pool bar, picnic tables, corn-hole game, and
whatever happens to be outside the prohibitive pool fencing.

Siestas Cantina is splendid. It's well worth the walk, and
almost worth being relegated to the wrong side of the fence.
The sapphire-filled pool, water features, and rather spectacular Mayan pyramid towering over everything make it hard to
remain on the less-privileged side of the gate.

Sipping a second, perhaps a third Coronado Crush, soaking
my shins, I resolve to either stay at the Coronado next time, or
figure out some way to get greenlighted for this pool. A person
can go decades without dying for a swim, until you stand on
the edge of a pool with a Mayan pyramid waterfall flowing into
it, which you are not allowed to use.

Notable Potables

Passion Fruit Caipirinha
CachaÇa, passion fruit, lime, and sugar cane

Mojito Frambuesa
Raspberry rum, sweet and sour, guava, simple syrup, lime,
muddled blackberries, mint, and Sprite

Sangria Rioja
Cabernet, Cointreau, guava, agave nectar, passion fruit,
mango, and Sprite

Modelo Especial
12 oz. draft

Reef Donkey APA
16 oz. can

Disney's Fort Wilderness Resort & Campground

Since the completion of Disney's mind-blowing Wilderness Lodge, far fewer people explore, enjoy, or are even aware of the ol' Fort Wilderness Resort. Decades ago, the removal of the endearing River Country water park began a swift and steady decline, which the lodge accelerated, and has nearly terminated.

The Hoop-Dee-Doo Revue, novelty, and relatively affordable accommodations represent the meagre lifeblood through which the campground survives. It is a lovely addition to the resort; every bit as charming and authentic as Frontierland. To witness as this classic compound slips from memory, and perhaps the Walt Disney World map, causes heartbreak among guests familiar with the area.

The Chuck Wagon

You won't happen by the Chuck Wagon. You are either here in conjunction with Chip 'n Dale's Campfire Sing-a-Long, or you got lost on your way to the pool. When you find your way here, probably on purpose, you are having a good night.

The food isn't fancy, nor are the environs. It's why you're here, and not at the Swan or Dolphin. It all qualifies as comfort food. The setting is exactly what you would expect and want from a Disney-fashioned wilderness. There's a pond, enough pine trees to deliciously alter the very scent in the air, and Tillamook cheddar cheeseburgers. Most guests don't travel with the proper ingredients, so there's a kit you can buy to make S'mores.

Notable Potables

Smoky Mountain Apple
Ole Smoky Apple Pie Moonshine, Ole Smoky White Lightnin', apple juice, and cranberry juice

Robert Mondavi, Woodbridge Chardonnay, Cabernet Sauvignon

Sierra Nevada Pale Ale
16 oz. can

Crockett's Tavern

For most of my adult life, my love of the outdoors mostly exceeded my appreciation for a fine saloon. When faced with a novel outdoor activity, or an unfamiliar bar, I tend to favor the former. Crazy, I know, though those inclined to keep their loved ones engaged in their family vacations ought to consider it.

Had I ever come across a Disney-designed bar while camping, I suspect my loyalties would have been challenged. There's not a whole lot to it. I mean Crockett's is no Geyser Point. But since Disney put it together, and it sits here within a Disney resort property, it's just so darn charming. When there's a handful of Disney parks nearby, I become much less of a sit-in-a-bar kind of guy. Should I encounter a Crockett's Tavern out on the trail somewhere, I would surely hunker down, as it were.

Notable Potables

Black Smoke
Ole Smoky Blackberry Moonshine and Coca-Cola

Strawberry Lightnin'
Ole Smoky Strawberry Moonshine, Odwalla Lemonade, Monin Wild Strawberry, and Sprite

SweetWater 420 Extra Pale Ale
16 oz. can

Hoop-Dee-Doo Musical Revue
Pioneer Hall

If Big Thunder Mountain Railroad was sequestered in an un-Florida-like pine forest, far to the east of the Magic Kingdom, reachable only by bus and a sporadic boat, would you still ride it? You should, though it would be understandable if you skipped it. Hoop-Dee-Doo is similarly wonderful. Given its location, upon the road less traveled, it is a testament to the incredible spectacle of how popular it remains. Given time and room within your budget, this ought to be part of your Disney World visit, at least once.

You can drink here, or it wouldn't appear in this guide (I'm looking in your direction, Aloha Isle). Even if you couldn't, you should still go. It is an incredible family or date-night activity.

Not like anyone's floundering for something to do at Disney World, though sometimes we can use a break from nonstop attractions, churros, and Tiki bars (can't believe I wrote that).

The frontier feast and floor show has been a Fort Wilderness fixture since before I was born. While I don't properly budget for it anymore, financially or timewise, I recommend it to those who have yet to witness the consistent, hillarious performance. See it once. Carry its joy in your heart. Pass it on.

Notable Potables

Bear Republic Racer 5 IPA
16 oz. pour
Argyle Pinot Noir
Placido Pinot Grigio

Meadow Snack Bar

Walt Disney World is quite appropriately labeled a resort. Make that turn off the I-4 and you're instantly on vacation. Even before you get to any park, hotel, or immaculate parking lot, the lack of anything that is not entirely influenced by patent Disney brilliance transports you to another world.

Underlying, on top of, and ingrained in the glorious grounds is the fabled, undeniable Disney magic. It's what brings us, in droves. What keeps Disney on our minds, what makes you long for it two minutes after you've left, until the day you return, is the immeasurable creativity and care, the extra level of detail, the hidden magic.

It's the scent of waffle cones on Main Street, even when Plaza Ice Cream Parlor isn't open. It's emerging from the American Adventure theater right as IllumiNations is starting and finding a spot on the rail. It's Goofy's face traced on the pavement with water and a broom. It's the familiar voice of the public address announcer. It's a million things you don't think about until you walk right into one of them; it is that upon which Disney's creative forces spend their every waking moment considering and perfecting.

Meadow Snack Bar is one such glorious hidden marvel. It's a walk-up window, in the corner of a building behind the Meadow Swimmin' Pool. Almost no one not staying at Fort

Wilderness will ever see it. And, truly, most of them don't know about it either. Most guests are drawn instead, understandably, to Pioneer Hall. Anyone sitting beside the Meadow pool, who is suddenly struck by the urge for a refreshing beverage, understands hidden magic, and the true, unexpected joy of stumbling into a bit of it.

You don't expect such a place to carry your favorite pale ale. You would be pleasantly surprised to learn they serve margaritas. Faced with a menu, loaded with cocktails of which you've never heard, you'll pray to Brother Bear that pool water didn't short out your MagicBand. Finding each beverage is more perfectly suited than the last for leisurely consumption in the sunshine; you won't believe how far off the beaten path you have found your new favorite snack bar.

Davy's Lemonade, Strawberry Lightnin', Blackberry Colada Moonshine; one's mind starts to ponder how many days you have left, and who can you get to drive the golf cart back to your campsite. I had an entire day planned that did not include moonshine flights at the Meadow Swimmin' Pool. Happening across the menu board on the wall, I felt like Nicolas Cage's character in *National Treasure*, except with more depth and believability. My plans for that day promptly changed.

Notable Potables

Blackberry Colada Moonshine
Ole Smoky Blackberry Moonshine, frozen piña colada mix, and fresh berries

Strawberry Lightnin'
Ole Smoky Strawberry Moonshine, Odwalla Fresh Lemonade, Monin Wild Strawberry, and fresh strawberries

Michelob Ultra
16 oz. aluminum bottle

Trail's End Restaurant

A buffet that features eggs benedict, biscuits and gravy, smoked pork ribs, and a "Dessert Island" is well worth what it takes to get over here. Crockett's Tavern is right next door. If you don't have park tickets on this certain day, one might conceivably make a day and night out of this unlikely stop.

I would say you could throw in Hoop-Dee-Doo to satisfy the family, but who could really eat that much in a single day?

Notable Potables

Gullywhumper
Ole Smoky White Lightnin', BOLS Peach Schnapps, pineapple, and cranberry juice

Schöfferofer Pink Grapefruit Hefeweizen
16 oz. can

Disney's Grand Floridian Resort & Spa

The most luxurious of luxury hotels, Disney's Grand Floridian could make one forget there's a Four Seasons at Walt Disney World. (There is.) Those who stay here know what opulence looks, feels, and tastes like. I want one of these people to adopt me. Not confident I will ever stay here, I appreciate how they will let you stand in the lobby gawking at the vast vaulted ceilings, chandeliers, and gilded elevator.

The restaurants, food, and service are, of course, impeccable. What you'd expect, I imagine, if you owned your own cruise line; a cruise line designed and staffed by Disney cast members. The topic could fill an entire other guidebook, draining my savings in the process, so I shall, as ever, keep my focus on the lounges, bars, and beverages. Spoiler alert: they're amazing, too.

1900 Park Fare

I just said this isn't a restaurant review, but a serious guide can no more ignore Grand Floridian's fine dining than fail to mention the view and architecture. 1900 Park Fare is where you might celebrate Mother's Day, if you happen to be at Walt Disney World with your family over that particular weekend. It's a character restaurant, and boasts more children than a large elementary school. It's also a buffet. An amazing buffet. The kind of buffet you take your mother to on special occasions. You will want a reservation. You wouldn't try to take your mother out on Mother's Day without a reservation, would you?

Victoria & Albert's, Cítricos, and Narcoossee's are arguably more on the special side, but Mother's Day, in my family, always meant brunch, ice sculptures, and all you can eat. You may very well get all you can eat at the Floridian's three finest dining venues, though one is only open seasonally, and the others don't open early.

Any day of the year, a visit to 1900 Park Fare demands Floridian Strawberry Soup and Grand Mimosas. Truly, Park Fare has the one thing I look for in a restaurant, and truly the only thing any eatery needs: a breakfast burrito bar. Don't tell Mom it's the only reason you came.

Notable Potables
Grand Mimosa
Champagne, orange juice, and a splash of Grand Marnier

Beaches Pool Bar & Grill
If you're not staying at the Grand Floridian, you may be intimidated about entering a Grand Floridian pool complex. Worry not. The associated bars and quick-service counters welcome your custom.

We are not supposed to use the pool, but despite the grandeur and pristine grounds, they aren't that stuffy here. Don't make a scene, but you can dip your toes without fear of reprisal. Have a beer, and if you are truly going to try and swim, leave your sandwich on a table.

Notable Potables
Old Elephant Foot IPA
16 oz. can

Rekorderlig Strawberry-Lime Cider

Cítricos Restaurant and Lounge
I wrote earlier that, when it comes to Disney, you cannot have too much of a good thing. I stand by the statement, though I take issue with the presence of so many time-insistent lounges within Walt Disney World. I feel this way particularly since there is already so much to do, and there's never enough time.

To properly enjoy a quality lounge, one must, by definition, come in and stay awhile. Disney World has thirty or so such lounges. There are two on this property alone. Then there are a couple hundred bars, beaches, and patios, all demanding your attention.

I can bypass Cítricos because I'm cheap. You needn't follow me in this regard. If you enjoy fine dining, and already have your Epcot meals staked out, Cítricos is beautiful. Start with the view and work your way through the amazing menu.

Cítricos Lounge, though, is the exact type of place that ensnares me like well-appointed flypaper. I don't drag my family into such places, especially not when on a Disney vacation. When they are asleep, in the pool, or the arcade, or when I manage to leave them at home, I take up residence in the various lounges. I don't like to take up an entire table by myself, but I will. If I have to continue ordering dark beer, and pretending to work to keep a table without guilt, I will do that, too.

Notable Potables

Sempé Cocktail
Sempé Armagnac and Chambord, simple syrup, and lime juice

Nimbus, Vina Casablanca, Sauvignon Blanc
Glass/Bottle

Stella Artois
12 oz. bottle

Courtyard Pool Bar

Grand Floridian's Courtyard Pool is even larger and more glorious than the Beaches Pool on the BoardWalk. No surprise, since it's the Grand Floridian, and you're not paying for second best.

Notable Potables

Orange Blossom Pilsner
12 oz. can

Reef Donkey APA
16 oz. can

Gasparilla Island Grill

When first coming across this establishment, I had no idea what a Gasparilla was. Fearing it was a Disney character with which I was unfamiliar, I looked it up. Learning that

Jose Gaspar is not featured in Disney lore, I felt a bit better. Discovering he was a fairly disreputable pirate, I promptly went in and had lunch.

You can get a mudslide at any full bar or any counter that has the proper ingredients and a blender. It's hard to predict what you will find where. The Meadow Snack Bar, a walk-up sandwich window tucked behind the Fort Wilderness Campground swimmin' hole, has as many specialty drinks on its menu as 'Ohana. Gasparilla has mudslides. It's essentially a specialty coffee bar, and they must have figured, what the heck.

Notable Potables

Kahlua Mudslide

Bud Light
16 oz. aluminum bottle

Grand Floridian Café

Despite my 1900 Park Fare commentary, I am aware the Grand Floridian Café is a much more Mother's Day appropriate venue. The decor is exquisite, rivaled only by the menu. Children are far less likely to overrun the place. It does not have a breakfast burrito bar. I believe that ends the discussion.

As the mojito craze continues to exert itself, our taste for other beverages has mutated slightly. A creative and complex Bloody Mary mixture is something to be appreciated. The Stow Away Mary, at Epcot, with the chicken-nugget garnish, may be a bridge too far. Not to be outdone, the café's Chipotle Bloody Mary has your car keys in it. This one is a bit much for me, though I can understand ordering one, in protest, for the burrito bar disparity.

Notable Potables

Chipotle Bloody Mary
Chipotle-Infused Vodka made in-house, garnished with jumbo shrimp, chorizo, and a lime-salt rim

Florida Sunshine
A blend of Skyy Vodka, peach schnapps, Chambord, and cranberry juice, with a splash of orange juice

Mizner's Lounge

Similar to the understated and elegant Ale & Compass, at Disney's Yacht Club Resort, simply crossing Mizner's threshold transports you to another world of peace, serenity, and positive lounging. While living your life properly, you cannot but be passionate about Disney World. Sometimes, though, you just gotta get away.

Four theme parks, two water parks, the BoardWalk, Dole Whips, Disney Springs, forty or so hotel properties, with twice as many pools, miniature and standard-sized golf courses, boating, bowling, Hoop-Dee-Dooing, shopping, horseback riding, movies, Galaxian for the cool kids; it can get overwhelming. Mizner's is a perfect place to get away from your getaway, if only for a while.

When you come to a new venue, and there's a drink on the menu with the name of the place in it, order it. The Mizner Cooler, on paper, is a cross between a gimlet and a gin mojito. Don't ever order the latter, even with Nolet's Gin, unless you can monorail home. The Mizner Lounge makes everything taste good, even a combination of two drinks you don't really want.

The lounge is not open in the morning, and food service is limited. When available, take advantage of it, as they clearly have access to Cítricos' kitchen. As your wild day winds down, send the kids to Gasparilla for pizza, and sneak into Mizner. Curl up with a complicated cocktail. Ignore the television. Realize that you are blessed. A live orchestra plays nearby. You will be tempted to ask to have your mail forwarded. (Disney does not say no, often, but they will say no to that.)

Notable Potables

Mizner Cooler
St-Germain, Nolet's Gin, lime juice, simple syrup, soda water, and fresh mint

Salted Caramel Manhattan
Palm Ridge Whiskey, Carpano Antica Sweet Vermouth, salted caramel syrup, bitters, and pineapple juice

Narcoossee's

Like a spectacular view with your exquisite dining? Seven Seas
Lagoon resorts are lousy with them. The Grand Floridian has
a handful offering each. Victoria & Albert's may be the standard
bearer for presentation and service, though their best view is of
the kitchen. Narcoossee's cannot match V&A's elegance. What
does? For scenery, though, Narcoossee's stands alone.

This may be my own inability to grow up, but one of
Narcoossee's signature drinks reminds me of a Mind Eraser.
The Narcoossee Nutcracker has a few of the same ingredients,
and sparked a memory when I saw it. Of course, I had to order
one. It does not come layered, though it does have a straw.
Don't suck the whole thing down at one go.

Do you have a favorite wine? I am not sure that I do, though
every time I see Cakebread Chardonnay, by the glass, I have to
have it. That sounds like it might be my favorite, then, huh?
Every time *Young Frankenstein* is on, I have to watch it, but it's
not my favorite movie. It's not even my favorite Mel Brooks
movie. Besides, I prefer red wine. It likely has to do with scarcity. I don't see it a lot; *Young Frankenstein* and Cakebread, both.
So, when I do, I can't resist. Narcoossee's has it. Despite the
traditional upsell by the types of places that carry Cakebread,
it's not horrendously expensive here. It's best if you have it
before any cocktail that resembles a Mind Eraser. Trust me.
Frangelico can play silly-buggers with your taste buds.

Notable Potables

Cakebread Chardonnay
Napa Valley

Narcoossee's Nutcracker
Kahlúa, Baileys Irish Cream, Frangelico, Skyy Vodka, and
whipped cream

Victoria & Albert's

I have several confessions. To begin, I have only been here once.
That's okay, you say? You trust my judgment? Well, I didn't eat
in the restaurant, nor did I even sit down.

Anybody still with me? I love a place like Victoria & Albert's;
the design, the decor, of course the service and menu. I love

the very idea. I'm just not part of their key marketing demographic. I see "Sixth Course Selections" on a menu and I start looking for the fire exit.

They have wine. If you are not intimidated by the food menu, and are going to stay and dine, you don't want my help with the wine list.

Disney's Old Key West Resort

This resort represents a bit of a paradox for me. I've been to the actual Key West a number of times. I love it. The island of Key West is one of those places where you are overtly encouraged to take it easy. The consistently perfect weather; the slow, but still courteous service; how there's always way more people lounging than exercising. It's an island without guilt. Laziness is provincially rewarded. The primary activity is watching the sun go down with a drink in your hand.

At Walt Disney World, I am beset by exactly the opposite compulsion. I love it here, of course. I just can't relax. I block time for sitting by the pool, on select barstools, and in lounges numerous and varied, yet I suffer from the consistent pull of a thousand undeniable activities.

At Old Key West, the Disney eagerness wins out. I eat. I have a drink. I sit by and in the pool. I put my toes in the sand of the tiny beach. As for slowing down and letting the outside world pass as it may, not a chance. Key West is textbook Disney. It's every bit the glorious paradise it is designed to be. It's just surrounded by sprawling square miles of Disney, demanding your time and attention.

Good's Food to Go

Never underestimate any Disney creation. While other resorts may be content to hawk flat beer and tasteless sandwiches across their pool bar, Walt Disney World constructs full bars, with accurate, appropriate theming. The food may not mesh with your pool body, but you'll order and love it anyway.

There was a time when I would not consider ordering Harry's Hearty Breakfast Bowl on the same day I was also considering taking off my shirt. On my visit to Old Key West, I resolved to get the bowl and keep my shirt on. My priorities have clearly evolved for the better.

This has been addressed, but I love a good Bloody Mary. Good's features one that I didn't think I would want. I don't like mixing a super-premium spirit into a multi-ingredient cocktail. I've also mentioned that I do not recommend the Patrón margarita. Too many components mask a really smooth liquor, and you're left with a glass of juice. It may still be delicious, but does it have the taste and spirit of the Bloody Mary, margarita, or mule you were hoping for?

Old Key West boasts Ketel One in its premium Bloody Mary. Ketel One is wonderful. In my brief martini phase, I insisted upon it. In the Key West Loaded Bloody Mary, I can't imagine it. And this thing is loaded. To taste Ketel One in this cocktail stew, I presume you have to make it so strong you will mess up that day's theme park plans. This turns out not to be the case. It is strong. What worthwhile Bloody Mary isn't? It is not overwhelming, and is not simply aspiring to overcompensate. They've achieved an ideal mix. It's a little hard to sift through the garnish. I wasn't about to be the guy who asked them to hold the bacon. I'd sooner hold the vodka.

Olivia's Strawberry Lemonade is another pleasant surprise. It contains Patrón, among a wealth of additional ingredients. The juice here is complementary, rather than combative. It's a truly sweet drink, which does not appeal to everyone. It is an almost ideal poolside beverage, and the Key Lime juice is a nice touch.

Notable Potables

Key West Loaded Bloody Mary
Premium Bloody Mary made with Ketel One Vodka, bacon, shrimp, jumbo olives, celery, and limes

Olivia's Strawberry Lemonade
Patrón Silver Tequila, fresh Key Lime juice, strawberry, and Odwalla Lemonade with a sugared rim

Gurgling Suitcase

The name may give you pause, as will the bar itself. Had you a mind, and the willpower to hang out, this is where you should do it. Tiny, kitschy, difficult to find a seat; Gurgling Suitcase captures the Key West pub spirit perfectly. The fish smell isn't quite as strong, but it's there. You can add to it by ordering Grouper Bites.

Neither of the featured drinks, below, pair very well with food. Each go wonderfully with the setting surrounding the main pool, which is where you ought to end up, as every Gurgling barstool will be occupied.

Notable Potables

Sultry Seahorse
Amaretto, crème de banana, pineapple and orange Juices, and a float of cherry brandy

Turtle Krawl
Parrot Bay Coconut Rum, Siesta Key White Rum, Sailor Jerry Spiced Rum with grenadine, pineapple/orange/Key Lime juices

Olivia's Cafe

Olivia's is a delightful restaurant, with a Disney-charming backstory. It's essentially bracketed by two pool bars, so don't beat yourself up if you fail to make it all the way over here. The food is amazing, if you're considering it. The Seven Mile Sea Scallops dinner entrée comes with the only Polenta I ever liked.

Of particular note to me, Parrot Punch is on the breakfast menu. A strong drink in the morning is not necessarily a cry for help. As they say, the breakfast cocktail is the most important drink of the day. You can get a Long Island if you want, even where it's not featured, you just shouldn't. Parrot Punch isn't intervention-strong, though the combination of rum, liqueur, and schnapps will haunt you if you plan to park hop that day.

Notable Potables

Parrot Punch
Parrot Bay Coconut Rum, melon liqueur, peach schnapps, and pineapple juice

7 Mile Bridge IPA
16 oz. draft

Turtle Shack Poolside Snacks

Before my last "research trip," Turtle Shack was one of the few places within Walt Disney World which I had not visited.

It's not with the other Key West bars and eateries. I almost skipped it. It's a long way from the shuttle stop, and I was there at a particularly motivation-sucking point in the day.

Just hours earlier, I paid my very first visit to Geyser Point. I was never in danger of missing that; it was at the top of my must-do venue list. Settling in for an extended stay, I began to speculate whether anything was worth leaving here for there. Now, Turtle Shack is no Geyser Point, but it does have a delightful "local" craft beer, and that's instantly worth any side trip.

It's hardly in my nature to recommend a mini margarita. This uncommon offering might be perfect for those walking back to the lobby, main pool, or shuttle stop. Truly, it's too small to effectively get you back past the closest tennis court. If you had a cocktail at Gurgling Suitcase, then that IPA at the Turtle Shack, it might be all your brain and tolerance will justify.

Notable Potables

Key West Sunset Ale
16 oz. draft
Jose Cuervo Mini Margarita

Disney's Polynesian Village Resort

As a percentage of total guests at Walt Disney World, most of them, on any given night, are not staying at the Polynesian. Not a critique, it's just how the math works out. Most of the rooms are somewhere else. Given the theme, exceptional restaurants, resemblance to true paradise, and Dole Whip walk-up window, the Polynesian draws more non-guest guests than any seven other hotels and the Swiss Family Treehouse combined.

Figuring out what to skip, in favor of something else, is the blessing and curse of any Disney World visit. Never pass on the theme parks. Disney Springs and the BoardWalk warrant side trips. Time willing, take advantage of your hotel's pool. Rounding out the list of the absolutely necessary: the three resorts on the monorail loop, the Polynesian in particular.

Barefoot Pool Bar

Humble, rookie admission: my first time at Barefoot, I spent five minutes waiting for an opportune time to slip in through the pool gate. It goes without saying I wasn't staying at the Polynesian. Not until after I violated this long-standing Disney guest policy did I realize you can get to the bar from outside. I'm not proud of this.

For those truly staying at the island paradise, the blessings are too numerous to count. One for which I stand in envy, from the wrong side of the fence, is how your MagicBand gives you entry to the Polynesian's incredible swimming complex, and the much more attentively monitored side of the Barefoot Bar.

Those able to take a Pago Painkiller to a chaise, covered table, or into the shadow of the giant rock-slide are the envy of us all. A beverage on the dock can be similarly wonderful, if you aren't attacked by grackles. Still, it's not the same if you can't dip your feet in the pool, or your head in the waterfall.

I will try just about every margarita variation I can get my lips around. I don't even want to tell you about my first visit to La Cava del Tequila. Barefoot has a Niue Rita. Niue is an island in the South Pacific; I looked it up. This combination ought to convince everyone who samples it to eliminate sweet and sour as a margarita ingredient for the rest of their days. Fresh juice makes such a better beverage, especially with Cointreau. The Niue Rita has both. It also has my passionate approval. I can only imagine how much more I would love it with my lower half in the unattainable Lava Pool.

Notable Potables

Niue Rita
Jose Cuervo Gold Tequila with Cointreau and lime, orange, guava, and pineapple juices

Pago Pago Painkiller
Myer's Original Dark Rum, orange juice, pineapple juice, and cream of coconut over crushed ice

Kona Castaway IPA
16 oz. draft

Capt. Cook's

The Polynesian's answer to the resort food court. It could be difficult even to consider it surrounded by such exotic splendor and terrace restaurants. Those traveling with extended family will be overjoyed at the reasonable menu and the recognizable fare your children may more readily embrace. Grab-and-go sandwiches and beer will well serve those looking for a poolside or in-room retreat.

Notable Potables

Beringer White Zinfandel
Jose Cuervo Classic Margarita
Kona Longboard Island Lager
16 oz. can

Disney's Spirit of Aloha Dinner Show

This is an absolute party. I don't know if it is culturally misplaced to compare the luau to the Hoop-Dee-Doo Revue. I only do so to make the point that each is amazing. They are both a little pricey, but you have to treat it as the celebratory enhancement that it is. It's not simply dinner. It's not just a show. These are Disney-fashioned examples of the best of both worlds.

Yes, you can drink here. It costs more. Yeah, I know, but, if you're going to do it, you may as well go all the way, right?

Kona Island and Kona Café

A delightful two-sided spot to take in a meal at a resort that is simply lousy with them. Though similar, and adjacent, each has its own draw and character. Neither have the sought-after charm of 'Ohana. They also won't have near the wait, and, I'll say it, each has a comparable quality menu.

What Kona truly offers is a lesson in reading the fine print. You can eat at Kona Café regularly, and walk past it often, and still not be aware that it offers mimosa and Bloody Mary flights at breakfast. Upon learning this, I not only became a committed patron, I began to make similar requests every-where else. I don't speak to it specifically in this guide, though will tell you most Disney restaurants are not as enthusiastic about Bloody Mary flights as I am. And to the maybe slightly too diligent Cheshire Café cast members, I do not think Bloody Marys are inappropriate for yours, or any venue.

Notable Potables

Kona Cool Sundown
Blend of Vodka, Chambord, and cranberry juice

Mimosa Flight
Choice of three juices: orange, pineapple, cranberry, pink grapefruit, or liliko'i (passion fruit)

Gekkeikan Horin Junmai Daiginjo Sake
Glass/Bottle

Oasis Bar & Grill

With everything going on in the Ceremonial House and around the Lava Pool, it's easy to overlook the Oasis. As it's a pool bar, in paradise, I know how blasphemous that sounds. Whether you hop off the monorail, or walk over from the Transportation and Ticket Center, you aren't going to be drawn here.

There are wonderful salads, wraps, and seafood options. There's something called malasadas—Portuguese doughnuts with passion fruit. The full bar delivers a full complement of anything you want. And it's surrounded by a pool. Still, everything I got, I couldn't shake the compulsion to take it on over to the lobby, Lava pool, or Tiki Terrace.

Notable Potables

Pago Pago Painkiller
Myer's Original Dark Rum, orange juice, pineapple juice, and cream of coconut

Kona Koko Brown Ale
16 oz. draft

'Ohana

Do you have reservations? Then maybe never mind. Some Disney dining locations are so popular, they are more a point of interest than any mere restaurant. Even with reservations people often have to wait out front for a bit. Bless all of you who find yourselves in this situation and do not take it out on the assembled cast members at the bar and host stand who are truly not responsible for your plight.

Guests are welcome, though certainly not encouraged, to drop by and put their names in for a table. I personally would scoff at this practice, except Tambu Lounge keeps the same hours as the restaurant. One could do much worse for a waiting room.

Notable Potables

Island Sunset
Sailor Jerry Spiced Rum, Coruba Coconut Rum, and peach schnapps, combined with guava-passion fruit juice

Tropical Macaw
Coruba Coconut Rum, melon liqueur, pineapple juice, and cranberry juice

Pineapple Lanai

Why the Pineapple Lanai does not serve Dole Whip Floats with rum is beyond me. This is a more grievous offense than not selling them at Aloha Isle. Sure you can get yourself a Spikey Pineapple at Trader Sam's—except Trader Sam's opens about four hours later than Pineapple Lanai. Outrageous.

Tambu Lounge

Tambu is a Polynesian word that means "waiting." I don't think that's true, though it may as well be. Tambu is where Polynesian Resort guests gather as they wait for a table at 'Ohana, wait to check into their rooms, or, having already checked out, sit and wait for shuttles to take them mournfully back to the real world.

When not completely overrun by people expecting to be somewhere else, Tambu is an exceptional hangout. Pulled Pork Tacos, first of all. Then, the 'Ohana cast makes regular, musical appearances, and the air conditioning silences the guilt you're trying to ignore over not being outside.

You may not get a seat at the bar, and you needn't squeeze yourself into the tiny seating area beneath the television. As long as you are willing to go to the bar for your drinks, the comfortable accommodations stretching the length of the Ceremonial House's upper level are at your disposal. And, yes, if you've seen the menu, you read that correctly. There is a drink called the Backscratcher, which is garnished with an actual backscratcher.

Notable Potables

Backscratcher
Bacardi Superior Rum, Myer's Original Dark Rum, and passion fruit juice, topped with Jack Daniel's Tennessee Whiskey and a bamboo backscratcher

Lapu Lapu
Myer's Original Dark Rum and tropical fruit juices, served in a fresh pineapple topped with Goslings 151 Rum

Trader Sam's Grog Grotto and Tiki Terrace

As if the Polynesian Resort needs another vastly popular dining, drinking, and lounging attraction. In Trader Sam's Grog Grotto and Tiki Terrace, it's got two. The main draw, the theater-like grotto, is far too small. In a decade or so, Trader Sam's novelty will wear off, and the grotto will be a nice place to relax and have an interesting cocktail. Until then, it will be that place you hear about, read about, and where you may stick your head in the door. Enviously you may watch all the people who got there before you, and got seats, enjoying themselves thoroughly.

When Disney institutes FastPass+ for its restaurants, this will be one of the first places to get them. The drinks are intriguing. Service is outstanding. The decor is pure Disney. But you come for the show. If you are fortunate enough to get in, make sure someone in your party orders something from the specialty menu.

The right cocktail not only sends your head spinning in a delightful fashion, it affects the lighting, ignites a volcano, and can get you a spray bottle in the face. A dubious fate, perhaps. My preference is to order a Kona brew, and let someone else in my party trigger and endure the unnatural disaster.

As the grotto fills to capacity, as it will, invariably, make your way out to the terrace and some lighter-paced, open-air splendor. You can get all the same stuff, just without the electronic effects or cast member participation. You do get a lovely patio, when it's not too hot, or raining. There's also nightly live music. I love the mockup inside the grotto. I do not like waiting, or loitering around for a seat. With the humidity on the right side of tolerable, and a guitarist playing, I prefer the terrace.

Notable Potables

Nautilus
Barbancourt Pango Rhum, Appleton Estates Reserve Rum, Combier Crème de Pêche de Vigne Liqueur, tropical juices, and falernum

Tahitian Torch
ByeJoe Dragon Fire Spirit, tropical juices, passion fruit, and fresh lime juice

Kona Beer Flight
Three 5 oz. pours

Disney's Pop Century Resort

Every Disney value resort has a similar floor plan: lobby, shuttle stop, gift shop, several wings of theme-appropriate hotel rooms, whimsically shaped pools, some eye-popping stairwells.

Each has one food-court-type eatery and a pool bar. The restaurant is no drinker's paradise. Typically, you'll find a few varietal beers and some wine in a cooler. The pool bar maintains, though does not dramatically advance the theme, but did I mention it's a pool bar? It could be Lucy van Pelt's psychiatrist booth, and it would still be wonderful.

Everything POP Shopping & Dining

Seven stations of comfort food; unless you don't like soup, sandwiches, pizza, pasta, and ice cream. And, yes, the beer and wine are in a grab-and-go cooler. The best part about that, besides there being beer and wine for your consumption, you can take it out to the tables and chaises around the pool right outside.

Notable Potables

Woodbridge Cabernet/Chardonnay

Bud Light
16 oz. aluminum bottle

Petals Pool Bar

Unless you made a drink stop at Everything POP, and, even if you did, really, check out Petals Pool Bar; it's the pulmonary valve of Pop Century's beating heart. In contrast to

Walt Disney World's more elaborate properties, one common lament regarding value resorts is they have less to offer. If it has a pool, a pool bar, and an arcade with games from the 80s, I don't see a problem.

I bring up Black Cherry Lemonade elsewhere in the guide, almost as often as I mention not mixing complex cocktails with premium liquor. Flavored Grey Goose does not disappear within this recipe the way straight Grey Goose surely would. I also haven't determined what I feel is the best venue at which to enjoy this delicious drink. It's a nice problem to have, trust me. If Theme Park Press is willing, my next book will be *The Unofficial Drinking Grey Goose by Every Walt Disney World Pool Companion.* There will be a chapter on not drawing attention to yourself, so no one comes around to check your MagicBand.

Notable Potables

Apple Mule
Crown Royal Regal Apple, DeKuyper Pucker Sour Apple, and fresh lime juice, topped with ginger beer

Black Cherry Lemonade
Grey Goose Cherry Noir Vodka, Odwalla Lemonade, fresh lime juice, and grenadine, topped with Sprite

Disney's Port Orleans Resort: French Quarter

New Orleans is an exceptional vacation spot. The entire city oozes culture, adrenaline, and unfortunately, swamp water. Disneyland contains an extraordinary representation (minus the swamp water) in New Orleans Square. They've captured the positive essence of the food, mood, architecture, and ambiance. What's missing is the 4-for-1 happy hour, the olfactory presence, the overindulgence, and the inherent danger.

The Magic Kingdom has opted for Liberty Square, which is charming, and has its own appeal. For this lifelong Disneyland regular, it's just not the same. Thankfully, there is an entire two-property resort complex that's NOLA designed and dedicated. Again, it's clean, charming, entirely safe, and an attraction demanding a visit.

Mardi Grogs Pool Bar

If there's one thing the original New Orleans lacks, it's access to pool bars. Swampy water seeps into even the merest indentation; thus, there are few pools at ground level. The finest rooftop pools prefer you are a guest of those specific hotels, which is rather a lot like Walt Disney World, in fact.

Mardi Grogs is a perfect representation of what the real-world New Orleans is missing: strong drinks, undeniable humidity, a pristine pool that smells nothing like boggy wetlands. You're still not supposed to be in the pool without the proper MagicBand. True to the Big Easy, Port Orleans cast members aren't nearly as diligent as the Yacht Club in this regard.

The reason for concern: have you ever been to New Orleans? Excess seeps up through cracks in the street with the groundwater. Bars in the French Quarter, the real one, are open 24 hours. They close only when cleaning becomes an unavoidable necessity. The Disney version is far tamer, of course. In the spirit of authenticity, Mardi Grogs offers an All That Jazz specialty drink. It's a combination of three other weighty cocktails, and includes mango rum, midori, pineapple, orange, more mango, banana, cola, piña colada, pear, and raspberry. It's not exceedingly strong, alcohol-wise. With all the competing syrups and flavors, you will be relieved you are an entire boat and bus ride from the nearest attraction. You won't want to be on a roller coaster or within a spinning tea cup anytime soon.

Notable Potables

Front Porch Freeze
Cruzan Mango Rum, pineapple juice, and orange juice blended with mango purée

Gata-Melon Juice
Midori melon liqueur, pineapple juice, and Monin Banana, blended with piña colada mix

NOLA Cola
Cruzan Mango Rum, pineapple juice, and Monin Desert Pear, blended with raspberry purée

All That Jazz
A layered blend of the Front Porch Freeze, Gata-Melon Juice, and NOLA Cola

Sassagoula Floatworks and Food Factory

Essentially another food court, though this one offers fare with some local color. You can get pizza and hamburgers, though you can also, I should say instead, have gumbo, po' boys, and beignets.

As for drinks, it's really just a cooler with a few bottles. There is often a backlog at Mardi Grogs Pool Bar, for good reason. If you just want a beer or wine cooler, say, to take on your walk to Riverside, or to weather the line at the pool bar, Sassagoula has you scantily covered.

Notable Potables

Bud Light Lime
16 oz. aluminum bottle

Seagram's Escapes
Wild berries, orange sassy swirl, strawberry daiquiri

Scat Cat's Club

The pool bar shutters at dusk. Very un-New-Orleans-like. Fortunately, Scat Cat's Lounge starts revving up at 4pm. It has most of the same drinks and wherewithal, though the ten-layer All That Jazz may not have the same appeal out of the blazing sunshine.

With occasional live music, another few charming specialty cocktails, and several "local" Abita ales, you are much better off here than sponging for aluminum beer bottles in the food court or gift shop.

Notable Potables

Southern Hurricane
Meyer's Platinum and Original Dark Rum with tropical juices, topped with a float of Southern Comfort

Ambita Beer Flight
Amber, Turbo Dog Brown Ale, Purple Haze Wheat

Disney's Port Orleans Resort: Riverside

Many guests instantly favor the high-energy environs of Port Orleans French Quarter. I love it, too, especially the parts that closely resemble sections of Disneyland. If you favor Disney-fashioned serenity, and an arguably slower pace, do not overlook Riverside. When it's as hot as it was the last time I was there, I also recommend you don't try to walk between the two Port Orleans resorts. There's a boat. Get a beer from either pool bar, and wait for the life-saving watercraft.

Boatwright's Dining Hall

A fine dining establishment, with a level of charm and detail you expect in Epcot or Magic Kingdom. There is a boat hanging from the ceiling. Air conditioning accompanies the delightful, rustic setting. I recommend you also have dinner. At any rate, have appetizers and dessert. Crawfish Bisque and Crème Brûlée pair beautifully with the full lineup of Abita beers, and even a Sazerac, which I would be otherwise hesitant to order.

Notable Potables

Sazerac
Bulleit Rye Small Batch American Whiskey, agave nectar, and Peychaud's Bitters with a splash of Pernod

Abita Turbodog Dark Brown Ale
16 oz. draft

Muddy Rivers Pool Bar

This is where I first had SweetWater 420 Extra Pale Ale, and I am ashamed to admit it. Having wandered Walt Disney World for decades, having noticed SweetWater's availability for at least the last couple visits, I never tried it. It's not entirely my fault. Every time I saw it, it was sitting alongside something else I already knew I really liked. Whether Kona Castaway IPA at the Polynesian Barefoot Bar, Sierra Nevada Torpedo at Crockett's Tavern in Fort Wilderness, or Reef Donkey APA from Pretzel Palooza at Hollywood Studios, I have trouble passing up an IPA for a pale ale, even when it's extra pale.

I was a fool. I finally had one, even though Muddy Waters quite blatantly offers my much-loved Torpedo. It's now my second favorite pale ale. If Disney would carry Ballast Point's Grunion, I may order nothing else. Until then, SweetWater is a lovely find. I weep for the years I ignored it.

Notable Potables

Hurricane
Gosling's Black Seal Rum, Don Q Cristal Rum, tropical juices, grenadine, and Monin Red Passion Fruit, topped with a float of Gosling's Black Seal Rum

SweetWater 420 Extra Pale Ale
16 oz. can

River Roost

Another venue well-suited to sipping Sazerac. I, of course, had a beer. Truly, I had a couple beers. You ought to be full from Boatwright's Crawfish. In case you're not, Colonel Peace's Pieces (more crawfish) is not to be missed. There is ample seating in the lounge.

I did come in here one day before the Roost was open, to escape heat, humidity, and a humming-bird sized insect I was unable to identify or ignore. A lovely can of SweetWater in my possession, I took a seat at a table to organize my notes. Without provocation, Benny, a managerial cast member, passing by, asked me if I would like a cold glass.

These simple gestures are what distinguish the Disney cast on the whole. The ability to notice a guest, in a remote area of your hotel, and to be kind and keen enough to recognize a potential, unspoken need, and offer to remedy it.

Notable Potables

Ramos Fizz
Hendrick's Gin, fresh lemon and lime juice, and agave nectar topped with soda water

Southern Hurricane
Myer's Platinum and Original Dark Rum with tropical juices topped with a float of Southern Comfort

Riverside Mill Food Court

There are three better places to get a drink, all of which can be seen from Riverside Mill's front stoop. No one's fault, it's just a food court. When your other options are pool bar, blues bar, and smashing restaurant, you only choose the food court if everything else is closed.

Notable Potables

Arbita Beer Flight
Three 5 oz. pours

Blue Moon Belgian White
12 oz. bottle

Fat Tire Amber Ale
16 oz. can

Disney's Saratoga Springs Resort & Spa

A reasonable walk to and from Disney Springs, depending upon the specific location or your room, perhaps. You may not get the same Disney feel that surrounds some of the other resorts, and the resort apparently is not a huge draw for non-guests. It is a beautiful property, has a couple terrific bars, and is worth a visit, but I wouldn't leave Epcot to specifically come over here. I have no problem strolling or boating over if I'm already at Disney Springs, though.

The Artist's Palette

It's Saratoga's food court, and, no, not the reason you came over here—unless, of course, you found yourself at Disney Springs on a Saturday afternoon without reservations. At that point, an inside seat at a hotel food court doesn't sound so bad.

It's not The BOATHOUSE, but it beats waiting for two hours in the elements. There are some worthwhile items on the menu, and they have grab-and-go beer, ritas, and mudslides. Grab one of those, then see if you can get into the Turf Club.

Notable Potables

Kahlua Mudslide

Bud Light Straw-Ber-Rita
Cigar City Jai Alai IPA
12 oz. can

Backstretch Pool Bar

Another of Saratoga's many pool patios. Each is more subdued than the main pool by the lobby. At least this one also has a bar nearby, and it's a full bar, so you can get the Black Cherry Lemonade I won't shut up about. Unless you are a dedicated wanderer, or staying specifically in one of the Grandstand wings, I am not sure what you would be doing over here.

Perhaps there's a Drinking Around the Walt Disney World Pools game going on. Given the number of pool bars through-out the resort, this would be quite a challenge.

Notable Potables

Black Cherry Lemonade
Grey Goose Cherry Noir Vodka, Odwalla Lemonade, fresh lime juice, and grenadine, topped with Sprite
Samuel Adams Seasonal
16 oz. draft

Chips & Slices

There are two types of people in this world: those who can make a good Bloody Mary, and quitters. The former know that Absolut Vodka is one of the best and simplest ways to boost your Bloody Mary game. Chips & Slices, a semi-temporary drinks cart on the turn at Disney's Lake Buena Vista Golf Course, offers a wonderful Bloody Mary, and you don't have to be playing golf to get it. I discovered it while walking from Saratoga back to Disney Springs. They also have Belvedere. I'm not one to push super-premium vodka, but I know there are those who swear by it, and I was impressed to see it here, for a fairly reasonable price. It's like finding Gentleman Jack served on an airplane, for the same price as Seagram's. You are kinda obligated to get one.

Notable Potables

Absolut Bloody Mary

Rolling Rock
12 oz. can

Yuengling
12 oz. can

On the Rocks

While the Saratoga Springs property may not be brimming with Disney statuary or animation, the main pool is 100% Disney-resort delightful. There's a slide, loads of seating, and a bar. I didn't try the slide, since I wasn't staying here. I did stick my lower half in the pool.

Notable Potables

Apple Mule
Crown Royal Regal Apple, DeKuyper Pucker Sour Apple, and fresh lime juice, topped with ginger beer

Kona Longboard Island Lager
16 oz. draft

The Paddock Grill

Another Saratoga Springs pool, and I still wonder why most guests would ever even pass by here. The hours are really good. They serve a breakfast burrito. There's a water slide. It's about as far as you can get from Big Thunder Mountain, and still be considered on Disney property.

Notable Potables

Strawberry Colada

Bud Light
16 oz. draft

The Turf Club Bar and Grill and Lounge

It is entirely possible to love a sun-drenched patio bar and a close-quartered pub with equal enthusiasm. I know this, because I do. There are few pursuits I find as relaxing as lounging upon an open-air sundeck, with some manner of soothing beverage in my possession. I also appreciate it if there are free

tortilla chips on my table. I take similar, though distinct pleasure in sinking into an over-stuffed club chair, at the obscure
end of a darkly appointed parlor. Which mood I'm in mostly
depends upon the weather, and what manner of patio or pub
we are talking about.

The Turf Club perfectly captures my style of indoor venue.
Dark wood, tranquility, comfort, refinement, a view if you
want it, and loads of polish. There's a covered patio, and it is
lovely. When I am in a mood to be here, though, it's because
I want a padded seat, mahogany, and air conditioning.

Notable Potables

Three Minutes to Post Time
Bacardi Raspberry Rum, Blue Curaçao, New Amsterdam Gin,
Skyy Vodka, Sprite, and a splash of orange juice

Banfi Rosa Regale, Brachetto d'Acqui
Sparkling red

Blue Point Toasted Lager
16 oz. draft

Disney's Wilderness Lodge

My first visit to the newly "refurbished" Wilderness Lodge
was a joy and serious eye-opener. Attentive as I am, I assumed
I was well versed, or at least knew about every must-do Disney
attraction and point of interest, even those I hadn't personally
experienced. Stumbling into Geyser Point, about which I was
entirely ignorant, was a shock. I spent essentially every minute
I planned to dedicate to the lodge as a whole solely within
Geyser Point's glorious confines. I have a yearning to go back,
similar to what children feel between their first and second
visit to the Magic Kingdom.

Artist Point

Commenting upon the beauty of a Disney resort, romantic
vista, or restaurant risks redundancy. At any rate, this place
is beautiful. It's pricey. There's a dress code. I maintain that
neither of the two preceding factors is why I didn't eat there.
Instead, I blame Geyser Point, Space Mountain, and my own
poor time management.

Finding a completely unfamiliar drink combination that I know I will love, even just from reading the ingredients, is better than finding a twenty in the laundry. I tended bar for so many years, getting stuck in a nigh-unbreakable pattern, it's a delight to find a bright, unexpected light piercing the canopy. I came all this way to find something as simple and brilliant as a Lodge Fizz. I would never put the three ingredients that make up this drink on top of Grey Goose. Someone with more faith than I did it. They were right. I was wrong. I love it. It's sweeter than anything I would have at home. Here, on vacation, it's perfect.

Notable Potables
Lodge Fizz
Grey Goose Vodka, Triple Sec, cranberry juice, and Sprite
Argyle Brut Sparkling
Willamette Valley

Geyser Point Bar & Grill

Disney does such an incredible job creating and presenting its magical alternate universe that when they remove, replace, or even slightly alter some bit of it, the passionate masses have trouble adjusting. There are many lamenting the recent removal of Trout Pass Pool Bar. I feel a personal loss whenever a pool bar disappears from the earth. Losing a Disney-fashioned pool bar, from beside an otherworldly Disney resort pool, to make way for a day spa, seems an intolerable injustice. That is, unless you've ever gone over to Geyser Point, some twenty yards down the path.

Upon my first visit to Geyser Point Bar, I forgot Trout Pass even existed. That was surely a trend, and at least part of the thinking behind the reconstruction. Trout Pass was nice and convenient. It wasn't an ultra-comfortable oasis, with a perfect view from every angle, etched into the very side of paradise. Geyser Point is.

The bar and grill open early, and stay open late. Guests may take breakfast, lunch, and dinner here. It's almost unfortunate. Despite the siren song of the surrounding theme parks, it is difficult to ever leave Wilderness Resort, or this patio itself.

When you are in a position to guiltlessly enjoy eggs benedict and a Bloody Mary, together, you are already in a good place. Do so on the shores of Bay Lake, with birds singing just for you and a light breeze drawing you deeper into to that state of semi-consciousness which such confines tend to promote. It is almost reason enough to miss one's Space Mountain FastPass+ window. Almost. Luckily, the Magic Kingdom is a pleasant boat ride, and quicker bus trip, away.

Here one could be content with Bud Light Lime out of a can. They have it, though you needn't settle. Contentment is for people in less ideal circumstances. Anything less than elation misses the point of coming to an exceptional patio bar.

The beer, wine, and cocktails all taste better here. I have had Elysian IPA before. I really like it. Discovering it on tap at Geyser Point was like an early birthday present—not completely, as I had to pay for it. That is to say, pay for *them*. For all the beers I had. My attempts to muster a complimentary birthday cocktail met with a similar lack of success. As much as I like to say Banana Cabana, I didn't get one. I also resisted the Northwest Iced Tea. It's a Long Island Iced Tea with Cointreau, rather than triple sec, which means it's better. However, no matter your commitment to using your Magic Kingdom FastPass+, you start mixing IPA and Long Islands, even really good ones, and you likely aren't making it back to the park.

If I have a complaint, it's how it's difficult to see the TV from the fire pit. Between the view and general splendor, Geyser Point is the type of venue that does not benefit from having a television. I don't say that, ever. It's true of California Grill, it was arguable regarding my wedding, and it applies here. I could lounge on a cushioned Geyser Point couch, facing away from the TV during the Super Bowl, and not regret it.

So, yeah, Geyser Point is not perfect. The open-air design invites the starlings to get a little close and comfortable. Disney also won't let you sleep here; not overnight, or even a couple hours in the afternoon. I've tried. You know how hot Walt Disney World gets most afternoons? Well, given it's brilliant placement and construction, at 4pm, Geyser Point is nicer than my hotel room. Though kindly, regarding this matter, the cast members on duty were not entirely accommodating.

Notable Potables

Black Cherry Mule
Zodiac Black Cherry Vodka, fresh lime juice, and agave nectar, topped with Fever Tree Ginger Beer

Elysian Space Dust IPA
16 oz. draft

Roaring Fork

Even the palatial Wilderness Lodge has a grab-and-go food option. Disney understands its guests. When you can afford to stay in absolute luxury, it doesn't also mean you're keen to set your pocketbook on fire at every meal.

Roaring Fork was closed for refurbishment when I was there. The website directed guests to Geyser Point Pool Bar & Grill. It's excellent advice, and is where I was headed anyway.

Notable Potables

Blanche de Chambly Belgian White
750 ml. bottle

Fat Tire Amber Ale
16 oz. can

Territory Lounge

Given the presence of Geyser Point, I'm reluctant to advise anyone at Wilderness Lodge to go anywhere else. I am also aware how silly it would be, for illustration, to expect Magic Kingdom guests to ride Space Mountain all day, exclusively. There is room, space, and time for variety, even when we necessarily forgo an undeniable bit of brilliance to achieve it.

Territory Lounge is the epitome of comfort. It's not contradictory to say that about several of the many Disney lounge areas, though something about the rustic approachability sets this particular lounge apart. It's rather cozy. That is to say, it's kinda small. I didn't have any trouble getting a table, and wouldn't have been devastated over it anyway. It turns out I need almost no excuse to return to Geyser Point.

The food and beverage selection is wonderful. Turns out the lounge shares Artist Point's chef and creative expertise. I don't always eat while I am lounging, but I was aware of that particular culinary insight, and made a point of it here. You should, too. Even the simplest snack, marionberry-filled doughnuts in this instance, is otherwordly.

Notable Potables

Raspberry-Ginger Mojito
Finlandia Raspberry Vodka, ginger, mint, raspberry purée, and fresh lime juice, topped with coconut water

Moosehead Lager
16 oz. draft

Napa Smith Organic IPA
12 oz. bottle

Whispering Canyon Cafe

While this is primarily a drinking guide, I cannot encounter an "all-you-care-to-enjoy breakfast skillet" without making specific mention of it. Whispering Canyon has one on their breakfast menu, and I implore you to go get one. It's a little pricey for a breakfast item, but given the all-you-can-eat nature, if you approach it the way it's intended, it may be all you spend on food all day.

Whispering Canyon also serves Bloody Marys at breakfast. My friend Minder is going to kill me, but I don't think you should get one. In my experience a breakfast cocktail suppresses the appetite. It is a waste to cut your breakfast skillet enjoyment short, even for the sake of one of our species' best beverages. Order the skillet, drink water, come back later if you want a proper cocktail.

Notable Potables

Mountain Trail Cocktail
Troy & Sons Oak Reserve Whiskey, Chambord, blackberry brandy, and wildberry, topped with lemonade

Masked Rider Gunsmoke
California Red Wine

Full Sail Session Lager
16 oz. draft

Disney's Yacht Club Resort

Ale and Compass Lounge

The Disney website describes Ale and Compass: "Find yourself here for a beer! High-end liquors are poured at this nautical nook in the evening, along with cocktails. Enjoy light snacks with your spirits."

It is refreshing to see Disney embrace the fine pursuit of lounging. Beer, wine, and cocktails are sold throughout the resort, at hundreds of delightful locations. Outside of the International Food and Wine Festival, Disney doesn't go out of its way to promote pure drinking venues. You can't blame the world's premier family entertainment company for wanting to keep alcohol consumption on the relative down-low. It warms my tippler heart to see an area such as this, openly dedicated to the dwindling art of adult relaxation.

I enjoy a glass of wine. Still, it is rarely my first impulse when ordering a beverage. It depends upon my mood, the venue, and, surely, whether I am out wine tasting. The dark leather, cozy confines and eye-catching wine list here at the Ale and Compass are sufficient to steer me in the wine direction. I suspect, were I a Scotch drinker, that's what I'd crave. I'm not. At all. So, I go for wine here.

Notable Potables

Conundrum
California red wine

Amstel Light
12 oz. bottle

Captain's Grille

You aren't likely to crave a coffee cocktail in central Florida. It gets cold here sometimes, though most Walt Disney World patios, cafes, and pool bars are more suited to, well, pretty much anything else. Captain's Grille's dessert list commands you to have a true dessert drink. Gianduja Chocolate Cake, Cookies and Cream Brownie, and the chocolate or vanilla gelato pair with the Jamaican Coffee in a manner that will have you coming back for these specifically, and probably skipping dinner.

Should the weather be truly coffee-beverage friendly, taking this divine cocktail on over to Beaches & Cream Soda Shop ought to be high on the list of everyone privy to Beaches & Cream. Not for a soda, mind you. You've already got a drink, right? The Jamaican's specifically coffee-heavy influence commands procurement of a Fudge Mud Slide. Those who manage to resist Captain's compulsive dessert menu, and I don't know how you do, the Fudge Mud Slide will fill the void, and terminate your diet. Anyone staying at the Yacht or Beach Club wasn't going to adhere to any diet anyway. It's the cruel paradox between the incredible pool and the surfeit of irresistible restaurants.

A classic Bloody Mary might be the Jamaican Coffee's polar opposite. In light of Disney's specialty drinks Menu, available at Captain's Grille, a Bloody Mary might not even catch your eye. But, I do so love the classics. An Absolut Bloody Mary does not require crutches and window dressing. If it comes with chicken tenders, throw them on the floor (don't really do that). Appreciate that it will come with Tabasco, and pretty much only that. You will be able to taste the vodka, which is where most of your elaborate Bloody Marys fall short. I recommend Bloody Marys for breakfast, rather than with dessert.

Notable Potables

Bloody Mary
Tomato juice, Absolut Vodka, and Tabasco, with a celery stick

Jamaican Coffee
Myer's Dark Rum, Kahlua, and freshly brewed Joffrey's coffee

Crew's Cup Lounge

This is another example of exquisite Disney craftsmanship. The bar, menu, and, of course, cast members are as wonderful as you could want or expect. It is not my favorite lounge. I am an amateur sailor, at best, though I adore the theme.

My issue is, there are no windows. I don't always require a view, certainly not when in a pub sort of mood. And Crew's Cup Lounge is spacious enough not to give off a claustrophobic vibe. I think the true problem is this lounge's proximity to the Yacht Club pool, and the glorious BoardWalk. In this lounge you can't see any of it. There are times, places, and situations when I am perfectly content to be four-wall contained. Crew's Cup hasn't yet become one of them.

Notable Potables

Strawberry Julep
Maker's Mark Bourbon, muddled strawberry, mint, fresh lemon juice, and agave nectar

Anchor Steam Beer
San Francisco (12 oz. bottle)

Yachtsman Steakhouse

While I do like to sail, I'm not good at it, and I am surely no yachtsman. Those who are, likely appreciate a fine New England-style dining hall with an appropriate dress code. When I make a foray into this area, I am more typically dressed as someone trying to fit in at the pool, and hopefully not draw the kind of attention that gets one removed.

Yachtsman has my favorite Chardonnay, though I much prefer it at someone else's wedding or retirement party; somewhere, that is, where I am not paying for it. At Yachtsman, you pay dearly. If that is what you are after, here it is delivered perfectly, and would be well worth it.

Notable Potables

Cakebread Chardonnay
Napa

Boulevard Unfiltered Lager
12 oz. bottle

Lagunitas IPA
12 oz. bottle

Walt Disney World Dolphin Hotel

When I am near Epcot and the BoardWalk, I spend all of that time immersed in either Epcot or the BoardWalk. The Swan and Dolphin are glorious resorts, with several enviable eating, drinking, and lounging locations. Given their proximity to Epcot and the Boardwalk, I just don't spend a lot of time there. You needn't be like me. Branch out. Spend some time on the road less traveled, and discover splendor that many of us miss.

Cabana Bar and Beach Club

Exhibit A: Were it not for the surrounding, sprawling Disney theme-park-laden resort, Cabana Bar and Beach Club is the type of place I could spend all day.

Cabana, and similar venues, present a blessing and a curse. It's a patio bar with couches, next to a lap pool. If you don't see the problem there, you are more well adjusted than I. Faced with the glorious opportunity to stretch out and have lobster rolls, adzuki bean crisps, and a bucket of craft brew, I am going to do just that. I do not, then, appreciate the guilt inherent in being within view of those getting in an aggressive workout in the lap pool.

Montego Punch is akin to a mai tai. Further, it is similar to the type of extreme-octane beverage I tend to discourage at Walt Disney World. On your "no parks day," on a patio such as this, I'm not going to fault anyone for trying and loving this drink.

Notable Potables

Hibiscus Cooler
Absolut Hibiscus Vodka, PAMA Liqueur, Thai basil, fresh lime, coconut water, Jamaican bitters, club soda

Montego Punch
Appleton Jamaican Rum, Cointreau, Florida fruit juices, fresh lime, Jamaican bitters, Myers's Original Dark Rum Float

The Fountain

Assuming, from the name, this was some manner of Disney-designed soda fountain, I was wholly delighted to find that's exactly what it is. It's grilled cheese, french fries, and a particularly large milk shake; the ultimate comfort meal, available within the charming confines of a Disney World resort. Wrapped within the blanket of glorious childhood sentiment, I am not even ashamed to admit I ordered grilled cheese off the kids menu, for myself. There are often so many hungry children in the place, no one is going to know none of them are yours. I also went with the non-alcoholic shake, the first time.

Notable Potables
Strawberri Kookies
Strawberry Patch and Cookies & Cream Ice Cream, strawberry topping and chocolate milk, topped with whipped cream & Oreo crumbles with house vodka

Seasonal Craft Beers
16 oz. drafts

Fresh Mediterranean Market
Like a stunning view with your buffet? How about Ferrari-Carano vino or a Bloody Mary? You will find it all here. Fair warning: having a buffet at a Disney resort is similarly hazardous to drinking Long Island iced teas by a Disney pool. It is undeniably going to affect what you do the rest of the day.

"Fresh Mediterranean" surely refers to the decor and the lunch spread. At breakfast, this is what you'd look for in a last meal. With a buffet available, I fairly well never opt for the menu. Given menu choices of Southern Staple, Fat Stack, "Monkey Puzzle" French Toast, and a delicacy called The Whole Enchilada, I was forced to violate a personal policy.

Notable Potables
Bloody Marys
Mimosas

Lobby Lounge
Pretty much nothing can compete with the Contemporary's rooftop California Grill Lounge. I say pretty much, in deference to those who have visited Animal Kingdom's Nomad Lounge, and I will entertain arguments in that respect. Even though everything else is a step down, a Disney lounge is inherently wonderful, and there's no shame in settling for something just this side of perfection.

While I live for roof, patio, and pool bars, I am also lazy. A lobby lounge means every time I enter or exit the hotel, I am going to pass by, and probably through, the lounge without considerable effort. Having taken a liking to this Lobby Lounge's Double IPA, I'm fortunate it's not at the top of an escalator or staircase.

Notable Potables

Dark 'N Stormy
Meyers's Original Dark Rum and fresh lime juice, topped with ginger beer

Hercules Double IPA
16 oz. draft

Picabu

The Dolphin's answer to the resort food court, Picabu will satisfy any guest's grab-and-go needs. If you have a few minutes to admire the wall art, and get a proper meal, this unexpected spot helps partially fill a significant Disney World hole. There are far too few Mexican food spots the world over, except perhaps in Mexico itself. Everywhere else, and this certainly includes Disney World, could use more of them.

Loaded nachos. Modelo Especial. Open 'til midnight. You're welcome.

Notable Potables

Sangria
Tropical Red, Florida Citrus White

Modelo Especial
12 oz. bottle

Shula's Lounge and Steak House

For guests in search of an exquisite meal at Disney World, I hesitate to recommend anywhere outside of Epcot, Cinderella's Royal Table, or one of the hotels surrounding Seven Seas Lagoon. It can prove difficult to get a table at many of these. I still have trouble recommending a restaurant you can find out in the real world, even some place as well crafted as Shula's.

True, there are only a handful of locations, but when you consider there is only one California Grill, one Akershus, one Tiffins, Shula's is fighting for room on a highly exclusive list.

For stuffed shrimp, steamed asparagus, and an IPA in air-conditioned comfort, though, I will steer anyone who will listen straight to Shula's Lounge. It would make me feel better if I knew you had dinner at Biergarten, too.

Notable Potables

Mary Anne's Sparkler
Knob Creek Bourbon, Domaine De Canton Ginger Liqueur, orange sour topped with Prosecco, and golden sugared rim dusted with chocolate ganache

Kim Crawford Sauvignon Blanc
Marlborough, New Zealand

Todd English's bluezoo Lounge

An elegant watering hole. That's the official description of the bluezoo lounge, and that captures it perfectly. When pursuing entertainment or leisure activities away from the parks and pools, BoardWalk or Disney Springs are automatic destinations. What you miss is an off-the-path paradise such as this.

Most bars have many of the same ingredients. When you locate a lounge like this one that features Square One and Russian Standard Vodka cocktails, you have located a particular treasure. If one of these inspired beverages falls off the menu, as they may, beg the bartender to make one anyway, until they pass you off to the food and beverage director, with whom you may negotiate the reacquisition of necessary ingredients.

Notable Potables

Serenity
Square One Cucumber Vodka, St. Germain Elderflower Liqueur, muddled strawberries, basil, rosemary, and a splash of lime and pineapple juice

zooberry
Blueberry-infused Russian Standard Vodka, fresh lemon juice, and rock candy syrup, served with a twist

Walt Disney World Swan Hotel

In case the overt allure of a pair of elegant Disney hotels is not enough to draw you in off the BoardWalk, the Swan joins the Dolphin with another bevy of lounges and pool bars that ought to garner your interest. Every step one takes in the opposite direction of Epcot is rightly excruciating. Eye-popping architecture, exquisite eating and drinking, and a vast pool patio complex will help make the side trip worthwhile.

Garden Grove

You needn't be at, or anywhere near, the parks to enjoy the Disney character experience. Even a way out-of-the-way cafe at a distant, detached hotel can put on a loyal spectacle. You'll also be thankful the Swan's Garden Grove upholds the traditional full-bar service. There is a more peaceful garden setting for those traveling without children, or if you've simply had your fill of mirth.

Notable Potables

Raspberry Bellini
Fresh raspberry purée, Prosecco, and Stoli Raz Vodka

Unita Baba Black Lager
12 oz. bottle

Il Mulino Lounge

My adoration for Disney lounges is well documented. In Il Mulino we have another fine example of the species. For me, this particular lounge presents a bit of a paradox. The barstools all face inward. This is not atypical. Many bar patrons favor, indeed seek out this manner of oblivion. Unless there is a vast expanse beyond and visible from the bar, I don't usually take such seats. Bartenders are some of my favorite people, yet I often crave more distraction to draw and occupy my attention.

The cocktail tables are more my speed. They are of a height I prefer in a bar table, and you can look out in any direction. My undeniable favorite, aside from a swim-up bar, is a couch. Il Mulino has a few of them. They are set up for parties of up to six. I am not the type to take up such room by myself, unless the place is desolately empty. I suspect Il Mulino is rarely so. It wasn't while I was there. I made due at a table, covertly loathing everyone on the couches.

Notable Potables

Testarossa-Red Head
Ketel One Vodka, Grand Marnier, and cranberry Juice, muddled with strawberries and fresh basil leaves, topped with ground pepper

Kimonos Lounge

You will never find yourself lacking for activities at Disney World. You would have to be a moody teenager to even pretend to be bored. Well, leave them in the room and come to Kimonos.

When was the last time you did karaoke? They've got it here, in addition to an immaculate, comfortable lounge area. The hours aren't great, but maybe on your way to or from dinner, pop in for something exotic and humbling.

Notable Potables

Pears and Brown Sugar
TRU Organic Vodka, fresh lemon juice, and house-made baby pear purée, garnished with a brown sugar rim

Rouge Red Fox Amber Ale
Japan (12 oz. bottle)

CHAPTER SEVEN

Disney Springs

The revamped, revitalized, and ever-expanding Disney Springs is a marvel, worthy of your time and attention. A comprehensive written account of Disney Springs would read like several volumes of an encyclopedia. The repetitive nature of reviewing the many venues, though they be distinct and delightful, would detract from each, and fail to capture the novel Disney Springs experience as a whole.

We shall thus focus on highlights. True to the spirit of this guide, every at least semi-permanent location that serves alcohol, down to the YeSake Sushi kiosk by the bowling alley, is included. Rather than detail how each has wine, light beer, and chicken tenders, I focus on the matters of true import: number of patios, presence of a full bar, happy hour, and preponderance of IPA. For the record, we consider the free-standing kiosks with tables in the vicinity as having a patio.

Outdoor vending carts spring up from time to time, in semi-regular locations, which offer alcohol. Though they aren't listed here individually, keep an eye out for them. The House of Blues outside bar and patio is wonderful, but there's no need to wait for a beer if that's all you're after. Turn in any direction, there's likely a kid behind a cart just looking for someone to serve.

AMC Disney Springs Dine-In Theatres

Fork & Screen is the latest luxury in entertainment dining. I appreciate the convenience and decadence in seat-side service in theaters, and I love the option of having a beverage during a movie. But we may be carrying this thing a little too far. Guests who choose the dining option do so intentionally, though I wonder how being surrounded by others eating tacos and raw fish might alter the viewing experience. And I say this as someone who adores sushi and Mexican food. Still, a delightful way to spend an evening, if you understand what you're getting into.

Patio: no
Full Bar: yes
IPA: yes

Amorette's Patisserie

From the outside, you likely wouldn't expect this charming bakery to serve alcohol. Well, that's why we're here. For a nightcap, perhaps a second dessert, or just on your way back to your hotel, a little line at Amorette's sure beats waiting for a table somewhere else.

Patio: not really; there are outside tables nearby
Full Bar: no; wine, champagne, Bellinis
IPA: no

AristoCrêpes

Most of the Disney Springs food kiosks serve some manner of alcoholic beverage. Whether it be a single beer, or a couple types of wine, do not overlook a free-standing eatery with no line.

The smell of divine pastry may be enough to draw you over to the remote area where AristoCrêpes stands solitary vigil. A glass of wine and a savory cheese-filled crepe ought to send you blissfully off to that nap you suddenly cannot put off.

Patio: essentially, it's surrounded by patio
Full Bar: no
IPA: sparingly

B.B. Wolf's Sausage Co.

It may only have beer, but what more does one need with a bratwurst and cheese spätzle?

Patio: yes
Full Bar: no
IPA: occasionally, on rotation

Blaze Fast-Fire'd Pizza

For convenience, quality, and general contribution to the betterment of society, it's hard to beat Earl of Sandwich. Since you probably shouldn't take every meal on your Walt Disney World vacation from the same place, Blaze is a similarly wonderful option, if with sufficiently different fare.

Patio: yes
Full Bar: no
IPA: yes

The BOATHOUSE

Those enjoying their lives properly have a healthy appreciation for open-air dining. Disney Springs is loaded with patio bars, patio lounges, and dining rooms with entire walls missing. The BOATHOUSE contains prime examples of each. The service and food are also exemplary.

Patio: indeed
Happy Hour: yes
Full Bar: several
IPA: many

Bongos Cuban Café

Excellent, inspired cuisine. Regular entertainment, and a wealth of options for hanging out over drinks. It ain't cheap, and can be a little overwhelming for some tastes. Don't feel guilty if you don't find Bongos relaxing. As any place serving a $55 pitcher of mojitos will tell you, that's not really the point.

Patio: yes
Happy Hour: yes
Full Bar: several
IPA: yes

Coca-Cola Store Rooftop Beverage Bar

Ever had a question you were too afraid to ask? An inquiry, the answer to which would be so difficult to believe, you don't dare even broach it? For those who have always wondered, but are afraid to ask, no, Epcot's Club Cool does not serve alcohol. The Disney Springs location, however, is loaded with it. Most of the offerings are not Coke-dependent, though I fail to see a huge problem with that.

Patio: yes
Full Bar: yes
IPA: no

Cookes of Dublin

When you find yourself deep in Disney Springs late at night, realizing it has been hours since you last ate, Cookes might well save your life. They do not sell cookies. You don't want to make that mistake when all the true bakeries are closed for the day. The onion rings are delicious, but aren't the healthiest midnight replacement for the cookie you were after.

Patio: yes
Full Bar: sort of, Raglan Road is right next door
IPA: no

The Daily Poutine

Do not dismiss any of the many seemingly obscure walk-up windows as a worthwhile drink stop. You can either spend a frustrated slice of your afternoon trying to get someone's attention at the giant volcano restaurant, or quickly secure a cocktail and a snack, hardly breaking stride, from a convenient, friendly, quick-service vendor.

Poutine has a lethal Fireball cocktail you should avoid. Most vendors, though, have far more sensible options for your consideration and enjoyment. Check them out.

Patio: yes
Full Bar: no
IPA: no

Disney Food Trucks

As much as I aspire to not succumb to the latest fad, since I'm far too cool for that, I do love the food truck thing going around. Convenient. Tasty. Aside from the bizarre $10 tater tots, the food is mostly reasonably priced. I defy anyone to walk past the food truck staging area, while they're open, and not get pulled in by the olfactory presence alone.

Patio: yes
Full Bar: yes, featuring Disney specialty drinks
IPA: yes

D-Luxe Burger

Speaking of fads, do we as a society really need restaurants specializing in $15 hamburgers? They're delicious. I won't deny that. The creativity is inspiring. But, the $15 burger then comes with nothing. Five dollars more for fries? Come on! I'll give them this, when the food is such an overt rip-off, the preposterously priced beer seems far more reasonable.

Patio: yes
Full Bar: no
IPA: yes

Dockside Margaritas

A sprawling patio, frequent live music, and a bar specializing in margaritas? If this place was located inside one of the parks, I would be powerless to ever leave it. The service is wonderful. It can get a little toasty at certain tables, at certain times of year. My heart goes out to the guitar player who was booked during the National Cheerleader competition taking place on the nearby Marketplace Stage. He was spectacular, though no match for the spirited, teen-driven spectacle next door.

Patio: absolutely
Full Bar: yes
IPA: yes

Earl of Sandwich

Food so good, I don't even mind that they don't always have IPA. This feels like blasphemy, but I don't prefer IPA when I am over-eating. One cruel joke Disney plays on guests of Harbor Blvd resorts: you can't participate in a meal plan, but you get to walk past Earl of Sandwich at least twice a day, on your way to and from your hotel. I ate there every day anyway. That'll show 'em.

Patio: yes
Full Bar: no
IPA: most often

Frontera Cocina and Express

Epcot and Coronado Springs are where you ought to go for Mexican food, though this will satisfy your craving. You have to pay for chips and salsa. I personally object to this, even when I understand the thinking behind it. A restaurant offering free food of any fashion is going to take a bath at Disney Springs. For the opportunity to sit in out of the elements and enjoy free snacks, even I would take periodic, excessive advantage of that. It still burns me.

The food and beverage selections are top notch. I just can't get past $4 chips and salsa. Offering Negra Modelo almost makes up for it. Almost.

Patio: yes
Happy Hour: limited time, $5 Margarita Madness
Full Bar: yes
IPA: yes

The Front Porch

Attached to the House of Blues, I mention the Front Porch separately as you don't have to pay to get in, and because it is such a glorious place to spend an evening, weather permitting. At that point in the night when the heat and humidity let up just enough to allow for outside seating, this is where you want to find yourself. Joyfully, it's also round about the time when the second happy hour session commences. Free live entertainment is another plus.

Patio: yes
Happy Hour: yes, two times daily
Full Bar: yes
IPA: yes

House of Blues

The bars, patios, live music, and cocktails are free-flowing and wonderful; one almost forgets this is a fine place to come have dinner. The full menu is inspired enough to pull you off the porch into the dining room proper. The exceptional service will compel you to come back. Between happy hour, dinner, regular concerts, then late night happy hour, if you by some stretch are searching for something to do, House of Blues invites you to make a night out of it.

Patio: essentially, yes
Happy Hour: yes
Full Bar: yes
IPA: yes

Jock Lindsey's Hangar Bar

Replacing a Disney favorite is a near hopeless task, even if it isn't purely Disney. Jock Lindsey's Hangar Bar had the auspicious honor of unseating a cult favorite in the old Adventurers Club. They wisely leaned on an icon in Indiana Jones, and kept at least a slice of the theme in tact. Jock Lindsey's may not yet be an equal success, but is a worthwhile, even enjoyable bar.

For any still upset over the Adventurers Club, you also got a Trader Sam's out of the deal. It's at the Polynesian Resort, rather than Disney Springs, though that's an arguable upgrade. No offense.

Patio: yes
Happy Hour: yes
Full Bar: yes
IPA: yes

Joffrey's

Another multi-faceted gem. At various locations at Disney Springs, and indeed throughout the parks, you will come across an apparently innocuous coffee cart. Many of them serve cocktails. No open bar, mind you. The offerings amount to a couple of specialty drinks, mostly involving coffee to some degree.

For guests traveling with others who do not share their appreciation for adult libations, the Joffrey's carts afford you the opportunity for discrete indulgence.

Patio: yes
Full Bar: no
IPA: no

Lava Lounge at Rainforest Café

There are days when no amount of shade, fans, or well-meant mist will salvage an outing at a patio bar. Lava Lounge has arranged a fairly advantageous setup, by remaining mostly covered, and the generous lake effect. When your previously enviable position at Dockside Margaritas becomes untenable, Lava Lounge makes a fine, shaded retreat, though it's pricey.

Patio: yes
Full Bar: yes
IPA: yes

Morimoto Asia

My love of lounging is challenged by Morimoto's unsettling concept. I am exaggerating. This massive, multi-faceted dining complex is extraordinary. There's just this Peking duck carving kitchen out in the open that unnerves me. The food, service, decor, and facing in the opposite direction more than make up for the carnage. (Specifically, baby pork ribs and "Bao Tacos.")

Patio: yes
Full Bar: yes
IPA: yes

Paddlefish

Come for the reputation, stay for the incredible bow bar and topside lounge. True to the overarching Disney spirit, Paddlefish is more than a restaurant, it's an experience. There's a view, which is rare for this part of the world. The service is, of course, wonderful, as is the menu. Then there are those chairs on the top deck.

Oh, what Disney could do with the Liberty Square Riverboat if they were so inclined. The Magic Kingdom alcohol ban is slowly giving way within its fine dining establishments. I think a restaurant on the *Liberty Belle* would be a welcome part of this natural progression.

Patio: yes
Happy Hour: yes
Full Bar: several
IPA: several

Paradiso 37

Three representative bar styles under one roof. A chic, interior, club-lounge type; one semi-enclosed, seemingly exclusive wine bar; and a wide-open patio bar. Yes, I know I'm leaving out dive bars, but no matter how creatively the Disney people might pull one off, it wouldn't quite fit the Paradiso 37 motif.

Each bar can get festive on any given evening. If crowds are not your thing, drift around the restaurant in search of more peaceful pastures. With several options, you just might find them.

Patio: yes
Happy Hour: yes
Full Bar: several
IPA: many

The Polite Pig

As an overt fan of barbecue and craft brew, I was delighted at the introduction of this particular restaurant. A convenient bar, right on the walkway, ushers guests in, and commands them to enjoy a lovingly crafted beer while waiting for their food.

Full-bodied beer does not necessarily lend itself to unbridled consumption of flame-grilled fare, though the combination here works without question. It may leave you with less energy than you might prefer, especially if your ambition is to return to the theme parks, though it is a wonderful problem to have.

Patio: yes
Happy Hour: yes
Full Bar: yes
IPA: absolutely

Raglan Road

This exceptional establishment warrants its own guide book. In the space provided, I must acknowledge my most aptly nicknamed friend, Raglan Randy Brutout. Randy's passion for the iconic Irish pub once prompted me to choose it over a day at Disney's Animal Kingdom. I don't encourage such behavior, especially on an abbreviated Walt Disney World visit, but Randy makes a compelling case.

With live music, exceptional beverages, staff, and character, Raglan Road is one of very few non-park points of interest I recommend without hesitation (see also Geyser Point).

Patio: yes
Happy Hour: yes
Full Bar: yes
IPA: yes

The Smokehouse

Another House of Blues annex, you may just find yourself running over here from anywhere in Disney Springs. They have happy hour, and an unexpectedly appealing beer selection for a walk-up window. And as a walk up window, there isn't any tedious wait for a table or particular bartender.

Patio: yes
Happy Hour: yes
Full Bar: mostly; no frozen drinks
IPA: yes

Splitsville

Far more than a bowling alley, Splitsville falls just short of a place for which I would leave a Disney park on purpose. When the parks are closed, I head here almost every night.

You certainly don't need to bowl to be here and enjoy yourself immensely—though you can, of course, and that's a blast also. It can be difficult to get your bearings, whatever you're doing. Fortunately, there are bars everywhere you turn. My favorite is the patio bar, naturally. I watched the Cubs win the World Series out there last year. I've never been glad to leave a Disney park, but the party going on for Game 7 on the patio validated that evening's decision.

Patio: yes
Full Bar: yes
IPA: yes

Stargazers Bar, Planet Hollywood Observatory

At Disney, I have difficulty directing guests toward an arguable chain restaurant. Disney Springs has several, and I also won't tell anyone not to visit them based upon my own personal inclination. If you have never been to a Rainforest, House of Blues, ESPN Zone, etc., or already know you enjoy such venues, they are worth checking out. Planet Hollywood, though, has a lot to offer, specifically to families, and may have exactly what you are looking for.

Stargazers Bar is a charming oasis amid the potential chaos of this massive restaurant, and Disney Springs itself. I tend to gravitate toward Splitsville to satisfy my indoor or patio desires, but nightly live music and a fine selection of craft beer have attracted me to Stargazers on occasion.

Patio: yes
Full Bar: yes
IPA: yes

T-REX

When Rainforest Café is too mundane, come here. Where the overgrown jungle restaurant leaves off, even more unreasonably large burgers and animatronic mastodons commence. It's much the same experience, if within a different epoch.

The intensity does not completely mesh with my penchant for lounging. It appears to be a fitting family dining experience, if the dining room, foyer, and waiting list full of families is any indication.

Come for the pterodactyls, stay for the volcanic dessert.

Gift shop: yes
Full Bar: yes
IPA: yes

YeSake

If you walk up to the shuttle stop to see your bus pulling away, you can make it over to YeSake and back, with a delicious beverage in tow, before the next bus arrives...most of the time.

Patio: yes
Full Bar: no
IPA: occasionally

CHAPTER EIGHT

Walt Disney World's Best Beverages

Le Geant Grand Marnier Slush

Les Vins des Chefs de France, France Pavilion, Epcot

Does a seemingly nondescript walk-up kiosk truly house the best beverage in all of Walt Disney World? Disneyland Resort guests, privy to the Cozy Cone, will caution you not to judge a cocktail from where it is purchased. The Cozy Cone is a delightful representation of its counterpart, in *Cars*, the movie, as is Cars Land in its entirety. You wouldn't take a date to eat there, nor would you expect that's where you may find the best drink you've ever had in Fillmore's Pomegranate Limeade.

The Grand Marnier Slush is another such hidden gem. Well, not so hidden. There was a time when guests could walk right up to the small outdoor vendor and purchase one with little or no waiting. Sometimes there would be some slack-jaw holding up the modest line, making foolish espresso purchases. Generally, though, the quick-service counter sat in adequate obscurity, especially considering the treasure housed within.

Now, and I point to the rash of drinking clubs, and Epcot's International Food & Wine Festival, the word is out. There's almost always a line. If it rivaled the wait for Frozen, or Soarin', or both, it would be worth it. The hypnotic orange creation, and the setting in which you may enjoy it, are a credit to the Disney resort, cast and spirit. Get a slush—Le Geant is the one with the extra topper of Grand Marnier—take two steps away from the counter, that others may get theirs, and embrace paradise.

I have enjoyed an exceptional glass of wine on top of the Contemporary Resort at sunset. I once partook in a bucket of cerveza on a beach by the BoardWalk, with my feet soaking in Crescent Lake (when we were permitted to do such things). I have been introduced to Nomad Lounge and Animal Kingdom's tangerine liqueur. This blended Grand Marnier cocktail, sipped blithely on the rail of World Showcase Lagoon, rivals them all.

Wild Passion Fruit Margarita
La Cava del Tequila, Mexico Pavilion, Epcot

That anything other than an IPA, or this exceptional margarita, tops a list of my favorite drinks is noteworthy. Like choosing between your children—you know you have a favorite—the task is as difficult to complete, as it is easy to second guess. Standing anywhere within or near the Mexico Pavilion, with a margarita in hand that perspires life-affirmation like condensation, one has to wonder if I've made the right choice.

You can't go wrong, really. I mean, we're talking about extraordinary cocktails at Epcot. What they've managed to accomplish, park wide, is incredible. It's why the scourge of drinking clubs is so prevalent.

La Cava del Tequila does have one advantage over the French quick-service counter: you may be fortunate enough to get a table, or a coveted spot at the bar. Then, if the La Cava cast isn't customarily overwrought, you can enjoy the company of some truly remarkable humans in addition to your outstanding beverage.

Tequila, ginger liqueur, mango, passion fruit, and lime juice, sprinkled with Tajín chili powder; if it wasn't so difficult to get the seat I love at La Cava, this margarita would appear at the top of every list. As there are times when it's difficult to even get in the door, I must give top honors to the French alternative that is typically easier to acquire.

Santa Monica Cider
California Grill Lounge, Disney's Contemporary Resort

It's no longer on the menu, but California Grill's well-staffed and appointed bar has all the ingredients and they don't mind making it—unlike Starbucks, where they take a rightfully dim view of those demanding pumpkin-spice lattes in July.

The degree to which the stifling climate at Walt Disney World takes visitors by surprise, then brings them to their knees, is stunning. Hyperventilating masses jockeying for precious, fleeting shade, and virtually bathing in the tepid drinking fountains, is testament to a race that woefully underestimates southern, specifically Floridian, weather. An inability to properly anticipate the elements can ruin your vacation. Except for about two weeks in January, heat and humidity are your principal antagonists.

From the Magic Kingdom, you are a mere monorail, boat ride, or mildly ambitious walk from three culturally distinct styles of luxury-resort relief. Sure, it borders on blasphemy to leave a park for any purpose other than heading to another park. Still, sometimes the elements are against you, and your sanity and survival are at stake.

Consider, 5pm on a blistering Floridian evening. You can either wedge yourself into the Tomorrowland Speedway line with a thousand of your closest, sweat-lathered friends, or you can ease into blissful air-conditioned comfort atop the Contemporary Resort, with a glass of sparkling refreshment and a stunning view of the Magic Kingdom. A Santa Monica Cider is strawberry, lime, agave, Hendrick's Gin, and at least twenty minutes of not standing in the sun.

The California Grill has a moderate dress code. When you see the place you'll understand. Also, unfortunately, it currently does not open until 4:30pm. If you are politely refused at the door, do not despair unduly. The Contemporary boasts plenty of additional restaurants, counters, and lounges, most of which employ hopelessly polite cast members who will be delighted to serve you Santa Monica Ciders to your flip-flop's content.

Elysian Space Dust IPA
Geyser Point Bar & Grill, Disney's Wilderness Lounge

A beer, within a short list of Disney World's best beverages, might raise eyebrows. To the incredulous, I say you need to develop a taste for IPA. Then, you need to have one at the Wilderness Lodge, lounging in the haven that is Geyser Point.

All IPA is not created equal. When you love a good one the way I do, and you find this incredible Elysian creation at a bar where you would live if Disney would allow it, Space Dust not only belongs on this list, you should serve it at your wedding, which you should hold here.

I referred to this earlier, but the confluence of Space Dust and the Geyser Point patio creates a vortex of wonderful with the power of an E-ticket attraction. I am not proud, but will again admit, slouching in a cushioned bear trap, beer in hand, breeze in my face, I nearly, consciously chose to forfeit a Space Mountain FastPass+. It took several starlings, dive bombing me, to bring me back to my senses.

Piña CoLAVA

Hurricane Hanna's Grill, Disney's Beach Club Resort

It takes something significant to stand out at Walt Disney World. Disney's Yacht & Beach Club does so, mostly due to its unrivaled location. It is bordered, indeed blessed by a luxurious, sprawling beach, mere meters from the thrilling BoardWalk, just around the corner from a relatively private entrance to, let's face it, Disney's best park, Epcot. It is the type of place where you could enjoy a simple cup of tap water.

That won't be necessary. The Yacht & Beach Club, and Hanna's Grill specifically, has terrific food and beverage offerings. The selection highlighted here is admittedly served throughout Walt Disney World, though guests will be hard-pressed to find a venue for which it is better suited. The CoLAVA Smoothie, an ideal blend of berries, pineapple, and coconut, makes a wonderful Polynesian Resort refreshment, is a true treat while strolling Saratoga Springs, and will bring tears to your eyes if you order one beside the Grand Floridian pool. While each offer their variation of lounge-chair, smoothie-ingesting nirvana, only the Yacht & Beach Club does so within cartwheeling distance of Epcot.

Sangria Rioja
Siesta's Cantina, Coronado Resort Pyramid Pool

Getting to the Coronado's Pyramid pool requires a little bit of a trek, even if you're staying at the hotel. If you're not, you aren't really supposed to use the pool. In my experience, purchasing a $9 cocktail earns you the right to enter the pool area, and the use of a chaise.

Don't let the name dissuade you. This is no typical sangria. Drink too many of them in the sun, and yes, you're going to suffer that headache. Still, this is not the hastily assembled bucket of after-thought wine and fruit you commonly avoid. Featuring Cointreau, guava, agave nectar, passion fruit, and mango, this divine creation is well worth walking that extra mile, and will have you coming back, especially when the bartender at your own pool fails to make it exactly the same.

Mango Green Tea Slush
Joy of Tea, China Pavilion, Epcot

The multi-faceted wonder of Epcot's World Showcase is difficult to describe or properly wrap your brain around. When it comes to food, features, or culture, it is even harder to pick a favorite. Immaculate and authentic Italian architecture, artisan French *glacé avec framboise*, moonlit margaritas in Mexico, Canada's now dearly departed Off Kilter, the magic springs forth from an ineffable combination of faithful and diverse detail. When in search of a mouth-satisfying World Showcase beverage, picking one is problematic, though impossible to mess up. The Mango Green Tea makes our list as it is wonderful, of course, and because we had to choose one more.

It consists of everything in its name, and if you like traditional Chinese tea, this is not for you. The Joy of Tea kiosk has the straight stuff, too, which you can enjoy while the rest of your party delights in slushy-fruit sweetness. There are those who like to take their meals, and even their soft drinks, comfortably ensconced at one of Epcot's many extraordinary table-service eateries. Here, too, you cannot go wrong, Though the true joy of World Showcase counter service is the freedom it entails. Sit by the lagoon with your new favorite drink, or amble along the esplanade. Pass through continents of culture as you contemplate whence will come your next creative concoction.

For those proceeding clockwise around World Showcase, Joy of Tea sits exactly where you ought to be finishing the to-go margarita you got in Mexico. If you double time it from here, you will be about done with your slush as you approach the American Adventure. If you get a Dasani from there, you ought to be sufficiently hydrated as you reach France. See beverage #1, above. Enjoy. You are welcome.

About the Author

Christopher Schmidt is a former Disneyland Resort bartender and author of *The Complete Guide to runDisney: Disneyland Edition* and the counterpart to this book, *The Unofficial Disneyland Drinking Companion* (both from Theme Park Press). If it involves amusement, attractions, athletics, adventure, and responsible enjoyment of exotic libations, you will find Christopher in the middle of it, eager to write and tell you all about it.

ABOUT THEME PARK PRESS

Theme Park Press publishes books primarily about the Disney company, its history, culture, films, animation, and theme parks, as well as theme parks in general.

Our authors include noted historians, animators, Imagineers, and experts in the theme park industry.

We also publish many books by first-time authors, with topics ranging from fiction to theme park guides.

And we're always looking for new talent. If you'd like to write for us, or if you're interested in the many other titles in our catalog, please visit:

www.ThemeParkPress.com

. . . .

Theme Park Press Newsletter

Subscribe to our free email newsletter and enjoy:

- ◆ Free book downloads and giveaways
- ◆ Access to excerpts from our many books
- ◆ Announcements of forthcoming releases
- ◆ Exclusive additional content and chapters
- ◆ And more good stuff available nowhere else

To subscribe, visit www.ThemeParkPress.com, or send email to newsletter@themeparkpress.com.

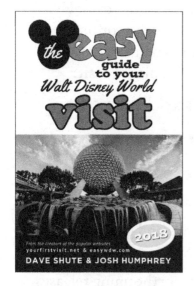

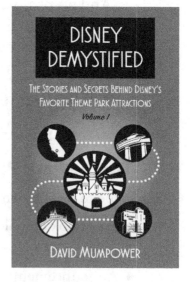

Read more about these books
and our many other titles at:

www.ThemeParkPress.com

Made in the USA
Las Vegas, NV
27 November 2023

81650278R00108